MARXISM AND EXISTENTIALISM

Walter Odajnyk, who is studying for a Ph.D. at Columbia University, was born in Ostrava, Czechoslovakia, of Ukrainian parents in 1938. With the aid of the U. S. Army, he and his family left Czechoslovakia in 1948, several months after the Communist coup d'état. After a year in Austria, they came to the United States, where Mr. Odajnyk received his education. He holds a B.A. from Hunter College and an M.A. from the University of California, Berkeley, where he specialized in political science and philosophy.

MARXISM
and
EXISTENTIALISM

by Walter Odajnyk

Anchor Books
Doubleday & Company, Inc.
Garden City, New York

The Anchor Books edition is the first
publication of *Marxism and Existentialism*

Excerpts from *The Marxism of Jean-Paul Sartre*, by Wilfrid
Desan, copyright © 1965 by Wilfrid Desan, are used by per-
mission of the author and of the publishers, Doubleday & Company, Inc.

Anchor Books edition: 1965

To
Taras Shevchenko
1814–1861
Bard and Prophet of Ukraine
On the One Hundred and Fiftieth Anniversary
of his Birth

FOREWORD

Aside from a good number of alterations, mainly of an editorial character, and a number of significant clarifications and additions, the substance of the work presented here was originally written as a Master of Arts Thesis in Political Science at the University of California, Berkeley, in June 1963.

I acknowledge with pleasure the undergraduate professorial tutoring I received with Dr. John Somerville, whose scholarly approach toward Marxism enabled me to grasp objectively its spirit and philosophy.

More directly, I am greatly indebted to Professor Sheldon S. Wolin, whose perceptive criticisms and elucidations of many basic arguments in this book have added to whatever merits it may contain.

Finally, I wish to express my gratitude to Professor Wilfrid Desan for his kindness in permitting me to read and make use of *The Marxism of Jean-Paul Sartre* while it was still in manuscript form.

W.O.

CONTENTS

INTRODUCTION

Sartre and Communism

Jean-Paul Sartre, the most thorough Existentialist critic of Marxism, oddly enough has taken it upon himself to serve as mediator between these two fundamentally opposed philosophies. This role appears to have developed from the fact that Sartre is a man of action as well as a theoretician. He maintains a philosophical premise which states that there is no reality except in action and that a man is only what his life is. Philosophically he believes that Existentialism provides a true interpretation of man and reality. But practically he concedes that Existentialism has no effective social theory and therefore can have little direct influence upon social and political phenomena. Yet Sartre as an existential man of action frequently takes direct part in social and political events. There is, however, no philosophical or logical reason why as an Existentialist he should favor the working class, or why he should be interested in acting in politics at all. A man may fulfill the requirement of defining himself in action and in life without necessarily acting politically. Political action in favor of the working class is with Sartre a personal choice, particularly since Existentialism as a philosophy is compatible with any and every social order and political belief. This has been amply illustrated in practice by the wide range of political commitments made by the various Existentialist philosophers, both atheistic and religious. The range goes from the approval of fascism by Heidegger, to the belief in democracy by

Camus and a number of other Existentialist thinkers, and to the defense of Communism by Sartre.

Sartre's choice of Communism for his political activity must stem partly from his experience in the French Resistance Movement during the Second World War when the French Communists proved themselves the best-organized and the most effective ideological and underground fighters. And partly, his choice is probably also determined by humanitarian and idealistic considerations which lead him to ally himself with the historically exploited and oppressed working class and to believe in the future ideal of a classless society, a society that supposedly only the working class is capable of bringing about. He has often implied and stated that socialism is the only hope for the future development and progress of mankind. And since the Communist Party is the only effective proponent of socialism he has given it his support. Nevertheless, his commitment is first of all to the working class and to socialism and only then to the Communist Party, and only as long as the Communist Party serves the interest of the working class and socialism. It is because of this idealistic and humanitarian commitment to the proletariat that Sartre has reserved for himself the right to criticize the Communist Party and even Marxism whenever he feels that the Party or the philosophy has failed the working class or has harmed the cause of socialism. It is also because of this commitment that Sartre has always maintained that the right to criticize Marxism comes only with a sympathy with its aims and the acceptance of its basic principles. The contention is somewhat self-righteous and similar to the argument of theists who claim that if one wishes to learn of God's existence one must first of all believe in His existence. The right of criticism cannot depend upon the acceptance of a principle but only upon the understanding of that principle, even though it may be true that a certain sympathy with the principle involved aids the understanding. But that is a minor point at the moment.

The important thing is that Sartre as an Existentialist has accepted the belief in the cause of socialism and has made an attempt at reconciling the most dominant philosophy of socialism with his own philosophy, yet always on the basis that such a reconciliation would aid the working class and the success of socialism. It is in this light that his writings on Marxism in relation to Existentialism must be read and understood.

Sartre's first comprehensive essay on the link between his philosophy and his political opinions was "Materialism and Revolution," published in *Les Temps Modernes* in June and July of 1946. The essay, which will be treated in detail in this book, expounds many philosophical arguments against a number of Marxism's major premises, including materialism and the dialectic. Yet during the course of the essay Sartre makes it quite clear that the criticisms are given only for the sake of improving Marxist philosophy so that it may serve as a more viable revolutionary weapon for the oppressed working class. And Sartre believes that Existentialism has much to offer to Marxism in this respect.

After a long silence on the subject, in the spring of 1957 Sartre published an essay entitled "Question de Methode" (or "Marxism and Existentialism," as it was called in the Polish magazine *Tworczosc,* upon whose invitation it was written). The essay presently serves as an introduction to the later published book on the same topic, *Critique de la Raison Dialectique.*

In the essay Sartre made a more definite commitment to Marxism by arguing that it is the only philosophy of the "rising class" and as such embodies the highest intellectual and practical truths of the modern historical epoch, and, therefore, that it is the only efficacious and realistic philosophy of our day. Existentialism with its emotional revolt against Hegel is but an appendage to Marxism. But after postulating these laudable claims for Marxism, he commences to criticize today's Marxism as an official, scholastic, narrow-minded dogma that has lost its force as a creative and living philosophy. And again he wishes to apply a dose of Existentialism in order to cure this official Marxism of its lethargy and ossification. He claims that the aims of Marxism and of his type of Existentialism are the same, but that Marxism has absorbed man and therefore lost him, and that Existentialism once more can lead Marxism to the man in the street, to the individual that Marxism has lost, yet whom it needs for the success of its cause.

Critique de la Raison Dialectique, published in 1961, is an attempt at such a beneficial merging of Marxism with Existentialism. The attempt, however, meets with failure, and Sartre proves only that the Marxists are correct in insisting that a union between Marxism and Existentialism is impossible. Sartre's attempt at a union of his two favorite philosophies will be discussed in some detail in the concluding chapter of this book.

Sartre's attitude of commitment and criticism toward the philosophy of Marxism is paralleled in his attitude toward the politics of the Communist Party and the Soviet Union. After the war he remained silent about the Soviet Army's forceful seizure of the Eastern European countries, about the 1948 Communist coup in Czechoslovakia, and Masaryk's "suicide," and about the Berlin blockade of the same year. But in 1950 he strongly denounced forced labor camps in the Soviet Union, claiming that there is no socialism where one out of every ten persons is in a forced labor camp. It could be said that until 1952 he was no more critical of the West and the bourgeoisie than he was of the Soviet Union and the Communists. But during 1952 and 1954 he published three articles on "The Communists and Peace" in which he laid the blame for the cold war on the militant anti-Communist attitudes of the West, and argued that the Communist Party, by desiring peace, was serving the best

interests of the working class, since only the working class
had nothing to gain and everything to lose through wars.
In 1953 his stand on the Korean War was ambiguous,
but in later years he placed the major blame for this war
upon Rhee, MacArthur, and the West. In 1956–57, however, he denounced the Soviet Union's intervention in
Hungary, calling the cause of the uprising and the subsequent intervention remains of the narrow Stalinist attitudes. But again he stressed that his denunciation of the
intervention and of Stalinism was motivated by the belief
that Stalinism and the unjustified intervention did much
harm to the socialist cause.

An objective observer could very well conclude from
all this that Sartre is perhaps a better Communist than
the Communists themselves in keeping the interests of
the working class and of socialism primary. His position
concerning the Communist Party as the only effective
voice and instrument of the working class and of the
cause of socialism has remained unchanged to the present. But one feels that the Hungarian Revolution was
somewhat of an awakening for Sartre, and since then his
enthusiasm and support for the official Communist
Parties and for the Soviet Union as the leader of the future socialist society has cooled to a considerable degree.
Where it is easy in the historical abstract to excuse and
even defend, as Sartre did, the Stalinist practices that
accompanied the building of socialism in the Soviet
Union, it is another matter altogether to be a living witness to the massacre by a socialist government of its own
workers who were struggling for a more lenient and perhaps a more true form of socialist government. Sartre's
commitment to the working class and to socialism therefore remains the same as before, but because of the Hungarian experience his attitude toward official Communism
is different. The initially non-Communist, moderate, yet
successful Marxist revolution in Cuba has provided Sartre
with another approach to socialism, an approach that does

away with complete dependence upon the Communist Party or the Soviet Union. In his book on Cuba, the description of Fidel Castro as the Existentialist man of action *par excellence* conforms well with Sartre's conception of the effective and practical union of Existentialism and Marxism.

Sartre and Camus

During the 1956 Hungarian Revolution and in his subsequent denunciation of the role of the Communist Party and of the Soviet Union in that revolution, Sartre certainly must have remembered the main historical and political problem presented to him by Albert Camus in the early 1950s. Since Camus and his philosophical differences with Sartre will be alluded to in the final chapters of this work, it would be well at this point to provide a more detailed background of these differences.

After the Second World War Camus came to be identified as an Existentialist of the Sartrean mold. There was a total agreement between them on all basic principles: both found existence to be absurd and man a possibility that was still to be realized; both argued that values must be created in life and not adopted *a priori;* both rejected absolutes and universals; both were atheists, yet humanists; and both placed the total responsibility for life in the absurd world upon the individual. In addition, there was a similar agreement between them concerning politics: they denounced bourgeois society and culture, economic exploitation, colonialism, etc. Actually, Camus never considered himself to be an Existentialist. Still, the broad philosophical similarities in theories and attitudes are much too great to be dismissed, and over his own objection, Camus must be dealt with as an exponent of French atheistic Existentialism. This does not mean that he has to be made to consent to all the details of the various existential theories. For a very basic disagreement between Sartre and Camus always existed, but it did not become evident until the publication of *The Rebel* by Camus. It was over this book and the ethical-historical views presented there that the now-classic debate between Sartre and Camus took place in 1952.

Ostensibly the debate began with a review of the book by Francis Jeanson of *Les Temps Modernes* (founded and edited by Sartre). The review's main criticism was that the book refuses to face historical reality and thereby serves reactionary forces. Camus, at the invitation of Sartre, replied, stating that the reviewer consciously omitted the main argument of the book, which instead of refusing to face historical reality refuses to accept the doctrine that turns History into an absolute and so justifies political absolutism, tyranny, and even mass murder. In his response, Sartre also failed to deal with this major theme of *The Rebel* and merely reiterated Jeanson's accusation. But the arguments did touch on many points concerning ethics, values, action, and politics, and they proceeded through numerous minor detours of a more personal interest to Sartre and Camus. Yet underlying the entire discussion was a matter that never came into the open: the old philosophical and ethical problem of means and ends. Both writers are anti-absolutist in philosophy and in politics, but Sartre leans more toward justifying the present means by the future ends, and Camus was more concerned with justifying the present means by themselves without recourse to ends whose effects are in the future and therefore problematical.

Camus had already illustrated his position on this matter in 1945 in *A Note on Revolt,* where he condemned the idea that the end justifies the means. Sartre, on the other hand, extolled the idea of ends justifying means through the character of Hoederer in *Crime Passionnel* (*Les Mains Sales*). Politically, this would indicate that Camus may be defined as the idealist and Sartre as the realist. And the political idealism of Camus is exactly the brunt of Sartre's accusation against *The Rebel* as a book ignoring historical and political reality.

Sartre has a point, for it is true that Camus placed his values in the subjective individual where they are not dependent upon action or history, whereas Sartre places his values exactly in the objective activity of the individual in history. The result is that Camus' values, which are independent of action, can always be more pure and clear than Sartre's values, which are created in the flux of conflicting and ambiguous action.

Camus, therefore, chose the uncompromising ideal and, with it, innocence; Sartre chooses the ambiguity of action and, with it, the responsibility for guilt and error. Camus' uncompromising attitude toward values was already evident in his early brush with Communism. In 1934 he became a member of the Communist Party in Algeria, but left the Party a year later because the Party line on a certain issue had changed in response to the political needs of Moscow. Camus could not sanction such political opportunism. After that, except for his Resistance philosophy of 1944, he always maintained that all political and social problems may be solved through tolerant and liberal democratic procedures.

With his emphasis upon the *means* in politics, Camus had to place his ultimate value upon the individual human life. This means that the preservation of an individual's life was the highest end for Camus, and he found few instances when this life could be sacrificed for some higher end. Sartre finds an individual's life expendable if in the end the utopian classless society is attained. Yet during the Hungarian Revolution this commitment of Sartre's must have undergone a severe test when he saw the utopian historical end used as a justification for the massacre of thousands of socialist workers for whom the future society was supposedly being constructed. He certainly must have developed a new respect for the position and the arguments of Camus. But one wonders whether

Sartre, if pushed, would not in the end argue that the more sordid events of the Hungarian uprising must be accepted as one of those errors that should be condemned but for which the responsibility must also be borne.

These, then, basically are the main positions of Sartre and Camus, their similarities, and their one major difference. It is the difference on the question of means and ends that should be recalled whenever the discussion that is to follow alludes to these two men.

Methodology

What is man? Who is he? What makes him what he is? What is his origin and his end? What does he know; how does he know?

The asking of these questions is one practical avenue of entry into a philosophy's basic world-view, for there is no doubt that the answers given to these questions will reveal the philosophy's most fundamental attitudes toward man's place and role in history, society, and politics. In determining an avenue of approach to a philosophy, allowance must also be made for its character. Thus an examination of the philosophy of Hegel and of most idealistic philosophies (roughly speaking, those that place spirit before matter) should commence with cosmology, for in their case an understanding of the general whole is indispensable to an understanding of man, who is part of that whole. With the philosophies of our concern, Marxism and Existentialism, the procedure should be reversed, for both of these systems of thought begin with the particular—matter, or the individual—and on it construct their cosmology.

The most fruitful beginning for this study, therefore, is an exposition of their epistemologies. There is also another reason for an introduction to the subject through epistemology. This is that even without a thorough study it is possible to surmise that many of the disagreements and conflicts between Marxism and Existentialism stem from their radically different conceptions of knowledge and consciousness. And thus, only when the "battle lines" are clearly drawn does it become possible to proceed to the main purpose of this work, which is the meaningful and critical examination of the interplay of conflicts and arguments between Marxism and Existentialism.

The Existentialism emphasized in this book will be that of the French atheistic school headed by Sartre. Most of the criticisms of Marxism made by this school, however, would be made by all Existentialist philosophies as well, in so far as the criticisms are existential and not external to the philosophy. All would, for example, criticize the Marxist view of consciousness and its deterministic conception of society and of the individual. But differences would appear in the nature of the critiques, for each critique would be based upon the particular characteristics of the Existentialist philosophy making the criticism. Thus a theistic existential criticism would be radically different from an atheistic existential criticism.

Because Existentialism as a mature philosophy is a later development than Marxism, and because of its interest in combating a philosophy which in its most major aspects is diametrically opposed to it, it is only natural that Existentialism has acted in practice as the protagonist and the challenger. This is especially true of French Existentialism, and this is an important reason why I have chosen it to represent Existentialism in the confrontation with Marxism.

The book, then, will retain this natural order, presenting the Existentialist argument first, and then the Marxist replies and counterarguments. Because of the difference in time between the philosophies, out of justice, the Marxist side must include the later orthodox developments of Marxism, in both the Soviet Union and elsewhere.

Also, throughout the discussion that follows, the reader should bear in mind an important historical fact. In the words of the political philosopher, Herbert Marcuse, both

Marxism and Existentialism have taken it upon themselves to provide a reply to the enormous question unknowingly bequeathed by Hegel—after his more mystical theories had been discounted—namely, if it is not the *Weltgeist* that guides history and man toward their fulfillment and essence, what does? In reply, Marxism and Existentialism have chosen the two opposing extremes of the spectrum, one assigning the role solely to society and the other solely to the individual. This original departure was and continues to be the major difference and the main focus of disagreement between the two philosophies.

As to the general order of the book, the first chapter provides brief outlines of the basic epistemological content of the two philosophies. And the chapters that follow each concentrate upon one specific area of conflict between them: materialism, the dialectic, an evaluation of one another as a socially effective revolutionary philosophy, general sociological and psychological criticisms concerning each other's origin and functions, and finally, the intricate matter of freedom, ethics, and action. In all these topics, I have taken liberties in developing and extending the arguments on each side as favorably and extensively as possible, given the framework of the theory. In other words, I have, so to speak, extrapolated when necessary each philosophy's basic statements and premises in order to aid its arguments and counterarguments and bring about a clearer confrontation.

Lastly, in the concluding chapter, aside from formulating a number of general theses based on the foregoing confrontation between the two philosophies under discussion, I delve to a certain extent into *Critique de la Raison Dialectique*—Sartre's most recent substantial work on the subject of Marxism and Existentialism.

Ostensibly this work was to embody the genesis of a philosophical union of the best elements of Existentialism with the best elements of Marxism. It is my contention, however, that this attempt at a union fails and that it

fails at the expense of Existentialism. For as the discourse
develops, the force and the logic of Sartre's own arguments lead him to forsake exactly those Existentialist
traits that he wished to incorporate into Marxism: the
subjectivity of the individual with the resulting humanism, and the individual's creative freedom in social, political, and historical events. To the end, Sartre makes
every endeavor to salvage the freedom of the individual,
but his own logic and arguments bury that freedom beyond any hope of a resurrection. And thus near the conclusion of his book he defines freedom in typically Marxist
fashion: loss of comprehension about nature and society,
its dialectic and movements, is the loss of freedom—or in
the more familiar Marxist formulation: freedom is the
recognition (awareness) of necessity.

In *Critique de la Raison Dialectique*, therefore, Sartre
undergoes a complete change in his outlook on such basic
concepts as freedom, conflict, society, the individual, and
the individual's role and place in society. The change is
away from the classical Existentialist views on these matters and closer to the Marxist views. In fact, on the basis
of the *Critique de la Raison Dialectique*, it is necessary
to conclude that Sartre is now a Marxist and no longer
an Existentialist. Sartre may object to such a classification, for it is true that his Marxism is of a peculiar Sartrean
mold; nevertheless, the dominant conclusions of his arguments are Marxist in character.

This all means that in the *Critique* we deal with a
totally different Sartre than the one described in the chapters that will follow. A great number of the arguments
posed against his former ideas and theories no longer
apply, therefore, when faced with his new views. However, their philosophical validity remains intact, for there
was no attempt on Sartre's part to give direct replies to
these arguments. He simply commenced a new and different train of thought that leads to new and different
theories, which in turn must be examined anew and

criticized from different standpoints. Yet there is no doubt that Sartre was prodded to develop these new concepts and theories because he found that his former Existentialist theories were at a loss for answers when confronted with exactly the type of arguments described in the pages that follow.

MARXISM AND EXISTENTIALISM

chapter one

MARXISM AND EXISTENTIALISM

Marxism

Marxism prides itself on its materialism: it is a materialistic philosophy, it claims.[1] The consequences for epistemology of such a philosophy are clear: matter is the basis of everything, of both life and thought. Thus Engels in *Ludwig Feuerbach and the End of Classical German Philosophy* consents to Feuerbach's basic thesis "that the material, sensuously perceptible world to which we ourselves belong is the only reality; and that our consciousness and thinking, however suprasensuous they may seem, are the product of a material, bodily organ, the brain. Matter is not a product of mind, but mind itself is merely the highest product of matter."[2] Matter is primary, consciousness and thought secondary. But the primacy of matter is in point of origin only, for once the mind is formed it can turn back upon the matter that gave it birth and even learn to understand its processes, its laws.[3] Armed with such knowledge the mind may successfully tamper with matter and influence its development and movement toward the ends that it desires.

However, this is jumping ahead somewhat. First the origin of consciousness must be accounted for more directly. It arises out of matter, true, but out of matter that has become transformed into a live organ—the brain. Next, the brain as part of man is acted upon by physical activities, particularly the procurement of food, and it is these activities that produce thought: "the actively working hand taught the mind to think. . . ."[4] And lastly, these

processes do not take place in solitude but are directly
influenced by society, in which man necessarily lives. His
social existence demands from him certain communal activities and interactions and in this manner communica-
tion, language—the instrument of consciousness and knowledge—is born. "Man is a member of society. Consequently
his consciousness is formed and developed under the determining influence of the social conditions of the life and
the activities of man. Consciousness is indissolubly tied
with language and from its inception has a social character. Marx wrote: consciousness from the very beginning is a social product and remains so, as long as men
exist."[5] Once consciousness is established in this way,
self-consciousness arises simply as the result of the consciousness turning back upon itself; it is not some new,
independent, or superior element.

But what is it that connects consciousness, the mind,
with the outside world, with objects? It is the senses that
perform this indispensable work. "Sensation is indeed the
direct connection between consciousness and the external
world; it is the transformation of the energy of external
excitation into a state of consciousness."[6] Without sensation consciousness could not exist. The senses carry the
impressions of the external world to the mind, and there
these impressions correctly *reflect* what the senses perceive. Marxists affirm that two qualifications must be
added to this correct reflection of the outside reality. One
is that the degree of representation may vary in adequacy,
and the second is that there is a difference between the
picture of the object in the mind and the object itself:
one is material and the other ideal, "but at the same
time," a Marxist writes, "it is somewhat like it." And he
continues, "this contradiction (difference together with
similarity) was emphasized by Lenin, who defined consciousness as a subjective picture of the objective world."[7]
The mind itself is a product of nature, and Marxism argues that it is therefore ideally suited to reflect this na-

ture accurately. (Of course, the power of the senses must at times be augmented by instruments, but that is a matter which does not invalidate the above ideas.)

All this should not be understood to mean that the mind is only a camera passively taking pictures of whatever the senses reveal to it. For the mind's ideal, subjective ideas of the external world are capable of being manipulated by man in accordance with his society's historically worked-out knowledge and experience. This experience is mainly found in language, which is an abstraction and as such independent of the objects, and their objective relations, in the external world to which it refers. But this independence is never absolute; in the last analysis it too is determined by the social conditions of life. It is from this socially given character of knowledge that all ethical, aesthetic, emotional, and intellectual concepts arise in man.

In the manner outlined above, Marxism solves the problem of ontology. Matter is the basis of all being; it is the only being, and the mind of man is an instrument which can grasp all being in its entirety. There exists no mysterious *"ding-an-sich"* which always escapes the mind. Things exist which as yet are not known, but which in principle can be known. Thus, playing on the Kantian terminology, Lenin says, "the development of consciousness in each human individual and the development of the collective knowledge of humanity at large presents us at every step with examples of the transformation of the unknown 'thing-in-itself' into the known 'thing-for-us.' . . ."[8] Practice—the acting upon the world—is the criterion for and the verification of our knowledge as well as the means of gaining further knowledge. It is practice, scientific experimentation, which turns a "thing-in-itself"—a thing not known—into a "thing-for-us"—a thing known to us. The proverb, "The proof of the pudding is in the eating" applies here almost literally. Materialism agrees, that is, takes the "naïve," every-day view of the common man concerning reality as the basis for its epistemology.

Since it is a fundamental tenet of Marxism that the world is matter, matter guided by definite laws, it logically follows that man, who comes from matter, is also subject to the laws of matter, in both his physical and mental structure. However, it has been shown that man does not live in the physical world alone: by nature he is also a social being. The society he lives in is similarly guided by and develops according to the laws of nature, but its laws differ qualitatively from the usual laws of matter. Thus in his body and in the most elementary aspects of his mind man obeys the laws of nature, but in the major aspects of his mind, in thought and in consciousness, he obeys the laws of society. These social laws are determined by the material processes of production and by the human relationships arising out of these economic occupations of mankind. The laws so determined have a forming influence upon all social institutions, relations, and even thoughts (philosophy, religion, art, etc.), and these in turn shape man's consciousness. The often-quoted passage from Marx reads: "The mode of production in material life determines the general character of the social, political and spiritual processes of life. It is not the consciousness of men that determines their social existence, but, on the contrary their social existence determines their consciousness."[9]

Man is therefore bound to act according to the two sets of laws: material and social. His existence and his behavior are in this manner "determined." The question of his freedom from these laws is senseless: what does it mean to be free of the physical causations which guide the functioning of his body? Any such attempts result in either disorder or disaster. The same applies, although in a modified way, to the laws that determine the functions of social life. A rational man will not seek to escape such laws but on the contrary will find the fulfillment of his freedom in conformity to the laws of nature and of society. It is in this sense that the well-known phrase, Freedom is the recognition of necessity, should be understood. Engels writes in *Anti-Dühring*:

> Hegel was the first to state correctly the relation between freedom and necessity. To him freedom is the appreciation of necessity. "Necessity is *blind* only *in so far as it is not understood.*" Freedom does not consist in the dream of independence of natural laws, but in the knowledge of these laws, and in the possibility this gives of systematically making them work towards definite ends. This holds good in relation both to the laws of external nature and to those which govern the bodily and mental life of men themselves —two classes of laws which we can separate from each other at most only in thought, but not in reality.[10]

The development of man and of his consciousness is thus complete. His origin is in matter. He gains consciousness by his physical activities in the world and in society. His mind, with the help of the senses, correctly reflects the world of external objects and its laws. Society forms the instrument of his consciousness—language; he thus begins to think and gain self-consciousness. The society he lives in is guided in its movements by definite laws which arise out of nature. These laws form the social institutions, relations, and ideas, which in turn imprint themselves upon man's consciousness and cause it to be what it is. Because this development proceeds in the same manner for all the members of a given society, the consciousness that develops in an individual is not radically different from the consciousness of other individuals living in the same society at a particular time. However, individual distinctions do arise as a result of the varying degrees of individual sensitivity and intelligence, and thus even in the perceptions of facts. Also, once society ex-

pands, a division of labor appears, giving birth to groups
with different relations to the means of production; consequently, new and more evident differences in consciousness arise among these groups or classes. But here too
allowance must be made for individual variations although
the general characteristics of the consciousness will be
stamped with the dominant class attitudes and interests.
It must be borne in mind that Marxism finds no universal
human essence applicable to all mankind, but it claims
that the essence of man is the result of his rearing and
life in a particular society and in a particular class: the
content of consciousness is not a universally given fact,
but a socially produced one. "The human essence is no
abstraction inherent in each single individual. In its
reality it is the ensemble of the social relations,"[11] says
Marx in his *Theses on Feuerbach.*

It remains to be added that all these phenomena are
dialectical: i.e., the development of nature, of society, and
therefore of man and his consciousness is a continuous
process still in motion and never terminating. This means
that the above phenomena constantly differ with time and
place. In this respect, all is relative and in a state of transition: matter, nature, man, his knowledge, and his consciousness. Also, the process is not circular or horizontal,
it is vertical, in the sense of a development from a lower
stage to a succeeding higher stage; it is a development
in quantity punctuated now and then by a qualitative
change, a "leap" from one quality level to a higher quality
level. This dialectical movement has no point of culmination; and with regard to epistemology it means that
the world can never be known with finality. Each age
must establish its own truths, its own facts, for these are
of the world and the world is dynamic. What was true at
one age or society may no longer be true at another age,
in another society.

Before proceeding to a brief sketch of the underlying
basis of the Existential epistemology, a serious qualifica-

tion of the above description must be given. It is a qualification suggested by Engels himself.

In one of his later letters Engels states that once man and society are formed, they both are in a position to influence the forces that formed them. This is a different conception of cognition, and particularly of freedom, than that outlined in Marxist theory, where man's entire consciousness and the whole social organization, institutions, and ideas, are determined by material and socio-economic forces. Engels dilutes the effect of this determinism and claims that the material productive forces are only the *"ultimately* determining element in history."[12] They are not the *only* determining factor. "The economic situation is the basis, but the various elements of the superstructure—political forms of the class struggle and its results, . . . also exercise their influence upon the course of the historical struggles. . . ."[13]

This matter becomes even more expanded when we take into account that, according to the *Communist Manifesto,* during the struggle between the bourgeoisie and the proletariat "a portion of the bourgeoisie goes over to the proletariat, and in particular a portion of the bourgeois ideologists, who have raised themselves to the level of comprehending theoretically the historical movement as a whole."[14] How is this possible if "it is not the consciousness of men that determines their existence, but, on the contrary, their social existence determines their consciousness"?[15] Now it is true that men may become conscious of the laws that govern social developments, including the laws that have a forming influence upon their own consciousness; they may become "socially self-conscious," so to speak. From this it would follow that they may also change their conduct to conform to the laws of reality, since true freedom lies in the recognition of and a conformity to necessary laws and facts. But if this is so, and it *is* logically consistent with the theory, then it is not strictly true that social existence determines

consciousness, as the theory also maintains. Given the
latter, one would expect a bourgeois always to remain a
bourgeois, since his education and his social relations
have formed his consciousness: but it now appears that
an escape is possible from the determining influence of
social existence.

Thus, by the dilution of the determining influence of
the economic factors upon society, and by the weakening
of the determining influence of the social environment
upon the consciousness of the individual, an unresolved
inconsistency arises in the theory, whose general tendency
is toward fuller determinism and predictability based upon
this determinism. This opens the doors to many different
types of interpretations of social and human phenomena:
if an economic or social cause cannot be found then another is equally valid. But then, this is no longer Marxism.

Existentialism

By concentrating on the Existentialist philosophy of the
atheistic French school this book seeks to make the confrontation of the two philosophies—Marxism and Existentialism—more meaningful and coherent than it would be
if the theistic Existentialists were included, since both
Marx and Sartre argue from the same general standpoints
—atheism and materialism—although their interpretations
of these concepts vary. Sartre's choice of atheism and his
rejection of Marxist atheism will be discussed in some detail in the second chapter, where it will also become evident that his materialism is a very general one—not granting to matter any causal laws and shaping influence upon
man's consciousness, but agreeing with Marxism that the
world is made purely of matter, there being no "spirit"
behind it. Thus Marxists cannot simply bring forth their
summary charge of "bourgeois idealism" against this form
of Existentialism, but are forced to find concrete issues
in their criticisms of it. Concomitantly, the similarity in
beginning principles provides an interesting observation

of how wide philosophies may range in their conclusions, even though they begin from the same general premises.

Existentialism is properly referred to as the philosophy of existence, or, more specifically, as the philosophy which claims that man's existence precedes his essence. This somewhat mysterious statement must be clarified. In its positive aspects the proposition means that even before man begins to look at the world and to contemplate it and to act in it as an individual he already exists. His contemplations and his actions are possible only because of his existence: existence, thus, is the first principle from which all else flows. It is only later, by living, thinking, and acting that man defines his nature and forms what is called his essence—that which he is and will be. From the negative aspect, therefore, the statement means that there is no such thing as a "human nature" or some other universal entity which could be considered the *essence* of all human beings. Every man is a *tabula rasa:* he is nothing that can be defined beforehand, but must define himself through his life.

Thus Sartre writes, "What do we mean by saying that existence precedes essence? We mean that man first of all exists, encounters himself, surges up in the world—and defines himself afterwards. If man as the existentialist sees him is not definable, it is because to begin with he is nothing. . . . Man simply is."[16]

But man is, only because he thinks; that is the second principle of Existentialism. The Existentialists have adopted Descartes' motto, "I think, therefore I am" and made it their own. This is the point of departure for any awareness or consciousness of existence as well as for all else.[17] For it is the only stable foundation, the only absolute truth that every man is able to discover. Therefore "every theory which begins with man, outside of this moment of self-attainment, is a theory which thereby suppresses the truth, for outside of the Cartesian *cogito*, all objects are no more than probable. . . ."[18] In other words, Existentialism proceeds from the subjectivity of the individual, but it claims that this subjectivity is the only objective fact in experience.

Existentialism has no interest and finds no purpose in a search for the origin of man's being and consciousness, for his ability to think. It begins with that which is given, and it studies the given, and it claims that one cannot study anything else but that which is given. How man thinks, whether from matter or spirit or anything else is a moot question. And Existentialism believes that even if answers are provided for such questions these answers can never be absolute, and they will never invalidate the main existential premise, that the only thing an individual can be certain of is his own existence.

Examining this remarkable consciousness of man—which originally is nothing and yet is so certain of its existence —it appears that the consciousness is bare even of an ego. It has no contents at all within it. "It is simply a spontaneity, a sheer activity transcending toward objects . . . a great emptiness, a wind blowing toward objects."[19] Consciousness finds its ego "outside," in the world with all other objects, objects which are "*for* consciousness, not contents *in* consciousness."[20] Sartre disclaims any representational theory of knowledge; since consciousness is an emptiness it cannot produce anything or add anything to that which it experiences. "When we see a mountain or imagine one, it is a mountain we are seeing or imagining, not our idea of a mountain."[21] Existentialism similarly does not "posit" the world: for the world is a material mass existing independently of man and his consciousness. As a matter of fact, this dichotomy between consciousness and the rest of the world forms another basic tenet of Existentialist thought: the *pour-soi* and the *en-soi*, the "for-itself" and the "in-itself." The *pour-soi* is that great wind—consciousness, and all else is *en-soi*. The *pour-soi* is the idealistic element and the *en-soi* is the materialistic element. However, the ideal element is dependent upon the material for its existence, but not in an organic sense. The *pour-soi*—being nothing, an emptiness, a void, or a "lack" as Sartre calls it—can find itself and exist only in its interrelation with the *en-soi*. To paraphrase a proverb, it must lose itself in the world in order to find itself in the world. It is the *en-soi*, the world of external objects, that causes the *pour-soi* to become aware of itself, first as a consciousness, then as a being, and lastly as a particular individual. Even if consciousness could exist alone—which it cannot—it could never attain to an awareness of its existence without the *en-soi*, which means without acting and interacting with the outside world. Therefore, "the *pour-soi is* only in so far as it is engaged in situation."[22] And it follows from this that "there is no reality except in action . . . man is nothing else but what he proposes, he exists only in so far as he realizes himself, he is therefore nothing else but the sum of his actions, nothing else but what his life is."[23]

It is exactly these characteristics of consciousness that account for man's absolute freedom and consequently for his absolute responsibility. The *pour-soi* is not only a void at its hypothetical conception, it remains so constantly; it is in flux, moving from one consciousness of *en-soi* to another consciousness of *en-soi*. Even its own past becomes engulfed by the *en-soi* and becomes an object like all other objects. And the same object-like character holds true for the future of the *pour-soi*.

The dialectic of present-past reveals the relation between the two realms of Being: the *pour-soi*, when it becomes pastness, is seized by the *en-soi* and rendered pastness or "facticity" as Sartre puts it. But since the present *is pour-soi*, a paradox is involved:

although we must define the present in terms of Being, whenever we attempt to specify the present, we are left with only an infinitesimal instant, a Nothingness. Here is the fundamental contradiction of existence: we always find the indissoluble pair, Being and Nothingness.[24]

Nonetheless, it is the combination of the past, present, and future and of the *pour-soi* which binds them together at each moment that gives rise to the Self. But because at each moment the *pour-soi* exists as a "lack" man is free. He is always capable of transcending and surpassing himself, and this he constantly does, for it is his nature to do so. At each moment he decides or chooses his present, his past, and his future. He is always projecting himself and losing himself, and it is to this dialectic that he owes his being. His destiny is never fixed; each moment a new future is possible. No determinism exists, for by natural definition "man *is* freedom."[25] There is only one matter in which he is not free and that is in his freedom. He did not choose to become free; he simply is born that way: thus he is condemned to be free. And being condemned to total freedom he is likewise condemned to total responsibility. Everything that happens to him, everything he does, is his alone. He chooses all that happens; there are no accidents, for he can always reject anything that is thrust upon him with recourse to the witness of his total freedom—suicide. If he chooses not to act, that too is a choice, and it is still his choice.

But even though man's freedom is unrestricted because there is no human nature or a universal human essence to curtail his movements, there does exist a "human universality of condition, . . . the limitations which *a priori* define man's fundamental situation in the universe."[26] These limitations are man's need to live with other men, to labor, and to die in the world. These, with man's freedom, responsibility, and the necessity of commitment,

are the only universals, and they therefore apply equally
in all times, places, and societies. But because all action
is by definition intentional, "no political or economic fact
can cause action in the individual. Motivation is inner."[27]
Therefore again in every respect, at all times and in all
places regardless of heredity, environment, history, society,
man is always free. All of this does not mean that he is
not influenced in his perceptions and in his emotions concerning the world by his birth, race, class, nationality, or
physio-psychological structure. He is so influenced. But
always he is able to transcend all these and to reject them:
if he does not do so, then he has chosen their influence.
In the end, he remains free. Freedom is his eternal and
indelible badge.

Because there is no God, a fact that French Existentialism chooses as an axiom without too much attention
to proofs, man alone must give meaning to his life and to
the world in which he finds himself. Sartre quotes
Dostoevsky, who once wrote, "If God did not exist, everything would be possible."[28] And Sartre claims that this
exactly is the starting point for Existentialism: everything
is permitted. And so it is man who is the creator of all
values; for by choosing certain values for himself, by implication he chooses them for all others also. Man is now
God, because he creates himself—he makes his own essence, and he also decides what values will be placed
upon his life and his actions and even upon the life and
the actions of all others. It is no wonder that anguish
comes to haunt him in this work, for he must make his
decisions alone without reference to heaven or to any
stable norms; and he knows that he alone bears the entire responsibility for his decisions. He is a God, but a
God chained; he is condemned to make these decisions.
He has not chosen to play God, and yet no matter what
he does he cannot escape his role. In the face of these
brutal facts the Existentialists can but speak of abandonment and despair: "I find myself suddenly alone and

without help, engaged in a world for which I bear the
whole responsibility without being able, whatever I do,
to tear myself away from this responsibility for an instant.
For I am responsible for my very desire of fleeing responsibilities."[29]

There is no doubt that for most men this is a horrible
freedom to have to face, and they continuously attempt
to escape it by the most varied forms of self-deception:
belief in God, in natural law, in the traditions and customs of the society, or in just keeping busy and not asking too many questions. It is the aim of Existentialism to
end such self-deception and to bring man out of his "false
consciousness" into the true realization of his existence—
which is freedom. The recognition of his freedom is the
highest value possible for man because it is the only factor that makes all decisions and actions in life meaningful
and truthful. It appears that the phrase made famous
by Hegel applies here also: freedom is the recognition of
necessity (in this case, the necessity is the fact of man's
freedom). The task of conversion from self-deception to
freedom is difficult, for in it is revealed the true nature
of man, which is freedom, and freedom brings with it
responsibility, and responsibility, as all leaders know,
brings anguish. Summing up all these threads of thought,
Sartre writes in *Being and Nothingness:*

It is precisely thus that the for-itself apprehends itself in anguish; that is, as a being which is neither
the foundation of its own being nor of the Other's
being nor of the in-itselfs which form the world, but
a being which is compelled to decide the meaning
of being—within it and everywhere outside of it.
The one who realizes in anguish his condition as
being thrown into a responsibility which extends to
his very abandonment has no longer either remorse or
regret or excuse; he is no longer anything but a freedom which perfectly reveals itself and whose being

resides in this revelation. But as we pointed out at the beginning of this work most of the time we flee in anguish and bad faith [self-deception].[30]

Until now the subject has been primarily concerned with the individual and the active characteristics of the individual's conscience. However, man lives with other men, a fact that even Existentialism cannot and does not want to ignore. In the same movement that the consciousness attains unto itself in the *cogito,* it also discovers the existence of others, as well as the fact that like the *en-soi* they are a condition necessary for its own existence. Being part of the *en-soi,* they too help to define an individual's consciousness, and it is in relation to them that a man is that which he is: as movement can be measured only in relation to other bodies, so the individual being can be measured only in relation to other beings. He cannot learn any truth about himself except through the aid of others. Also, in discovering the others, man quickly learns that they too are conscious and free as he is. (In this manner, and because of the fact that consciousness cannot be conscious of itself but only of that which is outside of it, the problem of solipsism is overcome.) An individual's consciousness is shocked into the realization that other free beings exist by their "look," for through it they invade his consciousness in a way that the rest of the *en-soi* never did. What is more, they deprive him of his absolute freedom in positing the world; and they even make an object out of him, for men can see and understand each other only as objects. They are *en-soi* to each other, never *pour-soi.* Still they are a free *en-soi* and as such they put a damper upon the individual's unlimited freedom. And therefore Sartre says: ". . . the intimate discovery of myself is at the same time the revelation of the other as a freedom which confronts mine, which cannot think or will without doing so either for or against me."[31] But no matter how it decides—for or against—the other is a constant source of necessary and perpetual conflict, never of harmony; for regardless of the relationship, whether love or hate, the existence of the other is always a restriction upon my subjective freedom. However, it is only a damper because the ability to commit suicide still attests to my total freedom. And if I don't want to commit suicide, then I have freely chosen this imposition that the other makes upon me. Nonetheless by making an *en-soi*, an object, out of me the other deprives me of my dignity as well; I appear as a means to him instead of as the end that I know myself to be. Yet given the ontological situation, the other cannot help but see me as an *en-soi*, and thus there is no way out of the predicament. This irrevocable ontological situation makes conflict, the natural state of affairs between every individual and all others, a veritable war of all against all.

Lastly, this entire panorama of the individual's rise into the world as a free being and his encounters with the *en-soi*, with matter, and with other equally free beings, must be viewed against the constant background of death. Death is the final point of reference for all life, for all actions and thoughts; it is the last great and total nothingness which annihilates any pretenses or roles that the individual played in life. In the face of death, men are but shadows, actors upon an ephemeral stage, and the drama they play is but a melodramatic tragedy—melodramatic to the eyes of the Existentialist because most of the actors act their roles in all seriousness, as if it were the true reality and not a play. For the Existentialist himself, with his recognition of reality, of death, the play is no longer a melodrama, but only a senseless tragedy. It is a tragic drama in which he is the star as well as the director and the author; the beginning is tragic since he is coerced to act his part regardless of his wishes; the middle is tragic since he knows that his past and present actions are but a meaningless prelude to the finale—which is death; and so the end is tragic since what once was a being has now become a void. And somewhere during the process man is asked to face this situation with courage, consider himself free, and even make an attempt at happiness.

Man's abandonment and despair are therefore doubly keen: not only does he know that he creates his existence through his own actions and that in these he alone must decide for himself and for others in all matters and take the responsibility for all these decisions, he also knows that in the end all his efforts are of no avail, for his existence and his being end in non-existence and non-being—in Nothingness.

This completes the very brief and cursory outlines of Marxist and Existentialist philosophies, outlines given mainly from the epistemological point of view. Since both are total philosophical systems, it is only natural that even an epistemological description reveals their attitudes toward many other matters, for in philosophies of this type all things are delicately interrelated so that it is impossible to speak of any topic in isolation from the rest of the system.

It is understood that a statement of a philosophy's position also indirectly announces which doctrines and ideas are acceptable and which are contradictory to the system and consequently false. Therefore, the basic disagreements and, as such, criticisms between Marxism and Existentialism are already visible in their broad outlines. They will form the major issues about which more detailed arguments will be developed. One such fundamental issue will be their contradictory views of the individual: Marxism claiming that the individual is a direct product of social relations, bound in his consciousness, thoughts, and actions to his society; and Existentialism denying that any deterministic elements operate on the individual, who by its definition is absolutely free. From these differing views on the individual, logical consequences follow for both

philosophies in their understanding of history, society, and
the individual's place and role in them. One sees history
as a large unfolding process guided by certain natural
(material and social) laws; it examines the historical progression from the primitive beginning and attempts to fore-
cast the immediate future development, always with these
laws serving as the basis of its interpretation. The other
looks at history and society as simply a chaotic mass to
which the individual must give some order and coherence,
somewhat in the manner of Kant; and it finds no natural
progression, but only the fact that the individual at all
times faces the same problem: the recognition of his freedom and his life in that freedom.

It is evident that this question of the nature of the individual really forms the central problem dividing Marxism and Existentialism on many other questions. But
there are also other issues, equally important philosophically, where wide disagreements are met with. Materialism, its validity and its use in Marxist philosophy is one
such issue, and it is to this that we now turn.

chapter two

MATERIALISM

The preceding chapter demonstrated in part that Marxism at its base is a materialistic philosophy. Materialism is its blood, and it builds the remainder of the philosophy with this element; in the final analysis it reduces all things to matter—society, history, and even the individual's conscience. The universe, from the minutest particles of energy to the most eloquent piece of music, is in one way or another the product of matter. Nothing outside of the material exists—neither the soul, God, nor anything else. Matter, however, is not just a shapeless, amorphous mass, but, as all can see, is capable of fine qualitative differentiations and operations. Also it is not chaotic in its existence, but obeys and responds to definite causal principles or laws.

Existentialism attacks the above conception of the universe from several points. Sartre finds that in its attempt to escape metaphysics, materialism falls into a metaphysics of its own: it uses the same criteria for its arguments concerning materialism that are used by the idealists whom it so much dislikes; it relies upon the principle of causality which is not a scientific principle, or at least a fact corresponding to reality, and in applying causation to social relations it often contradicts itself; and lastly, its materialism relegates man to the status of an object, a status incompatible with socialism, which is humanistic; and so from the beginning it ruins the very end it strives to attain. These criticisms must be discussed and elaborated upon.

Materialism is a metaphysics. Materialism denies the existence of God and of any transcendent finality. This is therefore "a clear and *a priori* stand on a problem which infinitely transcends our experience."[1] Existentialism also denies the existence of God *a priori,* but it does not deny that in doing so it is taking a metaphysical stand and not a scientific one.

In this connection, Existentialism also raises another question. It states that by reducing mind to matter Marxism is indulging in exactly the same practice as idealism when it reduces matter to mind. The statements, "Mind is the product of matter," or, "All things in the universe are a form of matter," are in the same category as the statements, "Matter is a product of mind (spirit)," or, "All things in the universe are a form of mind (spirit)." They are both *a priori* stands on an issue that experience does not definitely prove either way. All this leads Sartre to say, "I now realize that materialism is a metaphysics hiding positivism; but it is a self-destructive metaphysics, for by undermining metaphysics out of principle, it deprives its own statements of any foundation."[2]

To the above accusations, Marxism replies that Sartre is overhasty in his conclusions; it is exactly our experience and our knowledge of the world that give no cause for a belief in God or in anything else of a similar transcendent nature. Moreover, scientific anthropology and sociology can fairly well trace the origin of the major ideas of all religions—the beliefs in the soul, its immortality, and in a God:

> From the very early times when men, still completely ignorant of the structure of their own bodies, under the stimulus of dream apparitions came to believe that their thinking and sensation were not activities of their bodies, but of a distinct soul which inhabits the body and leaves it at death. . . . In an exactly similar manner the first gods arose through the per-

sonification of natural forces. And these gods in the
further development of religions assumed more and
more an extra-mundane form, until finally by a process of abstraction, I might almost say of distillation,
occurring naturally in the course of man's intellectual
development, out of the many more or less limited
and mutually limiting gods there arose in the minds
of men the idea of the one exclusive God of the
monotheistic religions.[3]

If from this evidence provided by science one concludes
that there is no God, where is the *a priori* stand? In this
fashion many more scientific conclusions of the above type
may be called *a priori* and therefore metaphysical stands.
These facts in no way transcend experience. On the contrary, they are verified by our experience of the world.

As for the mind and the universe being matter or spirit,
Marxism points to the facts of neurology and physiology
which undeniably demonstrate that the mind, and with it
the body, performs its functions in response to material
stimuli—chemicals, electric currents, etc. When Marxism
therefore claims that the mind has its origin in matter, it
does not indulge in the same unverified and unverifiable
thinking that idealism does when the latter affirms that
matter has its origin in some spiritual entity to which it
responds physiologically and psychologically. The only
conclusion that can follow is that materialism is in no way
a metaphysical doctrine; it simply interprets the world as
science has proved it to be: various forms of matter interacting with other forms of matter and giving rise to a
complex series of phenomena.

Not satisfied with the establishment of Marxism as a
metaphysical doctrine, Sartre next argues that materialism
is also only another form of idealism. Materialism claims
that the knowledge it has of the universe is absolutely
true, with all human subjectivity eliminated. And what
does such an absolutistic interpretation of the universe

imply if not idealism? In order to perform the trick of
eliminating human subjectivity, the materialist first makes
himself into an object, but then, instead of seeing himself
as an object moved about in the universe along with other
objects, he declares himself to be an *objective observer*
who can examine reality. As an object he claims to be able
to view the world objectively and in the absolute.[4] And
when his investigation is over, the result is the declaration
that "Everything that is rational is real," . . . and "everything that is real is rational."[5] This is Hegel, and Hegel,
the materialists agree, was an idealist. Sartre wants to
know where such rational optimism comes from, particularly since the world of the materialist is not his product
as it is Kant's, and since man can reflect only a tiny part
of it. That science finds some rationality in the world
does not permit one to conclude that *all* is rational. Also,
if human thought is a product of the world it may express
the world as an effect expresses a cause but not as a
thought expresses an object. "How could a captive reason," asks Sartre, "governed from without, maneuvred by
a series of blind causes, still be reason?"[6] Furthermore,
Lenin states that the reflection of reality by man's consciousness is " 'in the best of cases, an approximately exact reflection.' But who is to decide whether the present
case, that is, materialism, is 'the best of cases'?"[7] A proof
of its accuracy can never be found, for man cannot get
outside of himself. How then can materialism claim that
its conception of the world is absolutely true, or the only
true one, if its major and only criteria for the validity of
the reflection are internal and subjective: "its conformity
with other reflections, its clarity, its distinctness, and its
permanence. Idealistic criteria, in short."[8]

To all these arguments concerning its idealism, Marxist
materialism answers with *practice*: practice, the acting
upon the world and the receiving of practical proofs or
refutations of our actions. Our perceptions are not perfect;
the senses often deceive. However, activity is never de-

ceptive. If someone thinks he sees wood where there is water, let him try to set fire to it; if he sees water where there is fire, let him put his hand into it. The examples are extreme, for such obvious things as fire and water need no testing, except for children perhaps. But still, in less dramatic cases this is exactly the procedure by which our perceptions of the world are corrected and qualified; this is how men learn and gain knowledge of the world. Engels, again grateful to Feuerbach[9] in accepting the criterion of practice for the refutation of both idealistic and agnostic arguments, writes: "If we are able to prove the correctness of our conception of a natural process by making it ourselves, bringing it into being out of its conditions and making it serve our own purposes into the bargain, then there is an end to the Kantian ungraspable 'thing-in-itself.' "[10] Thus the verification of ideas in practice is not at all an idealistic criterion but a scientific and a materialistic one. Nonetheless, there is always room for doubt because knowledge of the universe can never be exhaustive and complete, particularly since the universe is never complete or stationary but is always growing and developing. Consequently the criteria by which it is known must change with it. This is another difference between materialistic and idealistic criteria, since idealistic criteria are static and permanent, and, as such, false to reality. If Existentialism is searching for an absolute to tack on to materialism, here is one: constant change and transition in the entire universe. Does this "absolute" make materialism an idealistic philosophy?

In reality, it is French Existentialism, which claims to transcend the duality of materialism-idealism, that admits the validity of metaphysical, and therefore idealistic, propositions. And it is Existentialism whose entire structure rests upon an absolute and idealistic principle: the unconditional freedom of the subjective individual.

As for the materialistic understanding of man's reason, Sartre does not do justice to materialism when he argues that reason is chained to all the causes that produced it. Reason is an evolutionary product of a mind which attained self-consciousness: a quantitative-qualitative development occurred within man's brain, producing a mind capable of reflecting upon its own actions and upon the laws that guide the world, and therefore even upon the world's development. This is no longer an effect expressing its causes, but an effect contemplating its causes and capable of acting upon those causes.

Speaking of causes, Sartre holds that there are no such things, or at least that they do not matter, that they have no influence especially upon the actions of men. Marxism, he maintains, is an *explanatory* metaphysics, for it attempts to explain social phenomena in terms of others—psychological phenomena in terms of biological, and biological phenomena in terms of physico-chemical laws, and in the process it rests upon the principle of causality.[11] But to its surprise, when it turns to science, materialism finds that causality is not scientific. Where, Sartre asks, is the cause in Archimedes' principle, or in Carnot's, or in the other abstract laws of science? "Science generally establishes functional relationships between phenomena and selects the independent variable that suits its purpose. It is, moreover, strictly impossible to express the qualitative relationship of causality in mathematical language."[12] And most physical laws are so expressed. The only reason materialism holds on to causality is its "metaphysical intention of reducing mind to matter and explaining the psychological by the physical."[13] And wherever this fails, Marxist materialism reverts to the dialectic; however, even this is futile, for the dialectic is a phenomenon completely different in character from causality: it is cumulative, whereas causation is linear. An example of such a resort to dialectic is the explanation of man's self-consciousness as a qualitative "leap" from one stage to another; in the process the linear causation is lost or somehow transcended.

Taking the alleged principle of causality from the material world, Marxism proceeds to apply it to society. And here again the principle runs into problems and contradictions. Thus the material forces of production supposedly cause the superstructure of culture, ideology, social institutions, etc., and these in turn cause the thoughts and activities of individual men. This is all very well, but it soon develops that ideologies are to a certain extent self-sufficient (Sartre adds, for the "purposes of Marxist propaganda"),[14] that men and their ideas can act against and contrary to what the superstructure should have caused. An instance of this type of activity was mentioned in the first chapter, where aristocratic and bourgeois intellectuals unite with the lower class and help to lead it in its struggles. What happens to causality there; what produces the autonomy of the substructure? The qualitative "leap" again?

Still another case of such a contradictory use of causality in Marxism is that, according to the theory, ideas, on the one hand, are caused directly by and reflect the social situation, and, on the other hand, also arise out of necessity, i.e., if a society is in need of an idea, an invention, or even a man, to solve some pressing problem, the idea, the invention, and the man will come. There has only to be a need. This means, in Marx's own words, that "Mankind always takes up only such problems as it can solve; since, looking at the matter more closely, we will always find that the problem itself arises only when the material conditions necessary for its solution already exist or are at least in the process of formation."[15] Or again, Engels writing in one of his letters claims: "That such and such a man and precisely that man arises at a particular time in a particular country is, of course, pure chance. But cut him out and there will be a demand for a substitute, and this substitute will be found, good or bad, but in the long run he will be found."[16]

But which is it then: ideas and men reflect and are

caused by the social conditions which are already in existence, or ideas and men arise as a result of social needs? Given the first theory as true, the last would be quite impossible. Instead of "needs" Sartre speaks of new social "tasks," and he states: "this means that the task even before it is carried out, *calls forth* the idea which 'will facilitate' its being carried out. The idea is postulated and worked by a vacuum which it then fills."[17] He attributes such a notion to the influence of the Hegelian dialectic. And he asks:

> Which am I to accept, a causal and linear relationship implying the inertia of the effect, of the reflection, or a dialectical and synthetic relationship which would imply that the last synthesis turns back to the partial synthesis which have produced it in order to embrace them and absorb them into itself, and consequently, that the mental life, although proceeding from the material conditions of society, turns back to them and completely absorbs them? The materialists are unable to decide: they waver between one and the other.[18]

Marxism answers to all this that it is impossible to hold a rational discussion with any philosophy that rejects the obvious fact that all events in the universe are caused. The universe is not a fickle woman who changes her appearance from day to day without some underlying reason or cause. Even the smallest particles of matter and energy have principles of operation according to which they act and react. Take away certain necessary conditions for the life of an organism, and it will perish; change the environment around a certain form of matter, and it will respond to that change. And in both cases, organic and physical, the response is always the same to the same stimuli and environment; it is not one response today and another tomorrow. This is causality, and it is upon this fact of the universe that science is built. Of course, causality is an abstraction to a certain extent, as is all language, and every scientific law or hypothesis. But it is a valid abstraction, a shorthand of what really occurs in the world.

It is not always possible to demonstrate all the causal threads, and it would be a superhuman task indeed, for the world is in this respect almost infinite in interrelations and interdependences. All that one can do, and all that science does, is to trace the several major causes of each occurrence. There are no unexplainable, which means uncaused, happenings: the explanation and the causation may be complex and intricate, but they are still there and can be discovered. If this were not the case, no science and no knowledge of the world would ever be possible. But history and civilization have demonstrated that knowledge of the world is possible, and therefore that causality is a fact.

As causation has been shown to operate in the material realm, its validity is likewise a fact in the human world of social and psychological phenomena. Social and human actions do not come out of a vacuum; they are determined by conscious and unconscious causes. It was Marx himself who discovered the motivating cause of social and historical life and development: struggle over the means of production. Once man discovers the causes of his actions or of social processes, it is possible for him to have an influence upon the causal reality and, in turn, upon the ends it produces. The recognition of the causal laws gives man the freedom to act upon those laws and to alter them to suit his purposes. Therefore, there is nothing mysterious about the superstructure enjoying an independence of its material causes and reacting back upon those causes.[19] Both of these matters, the ability of man to make the laws of nature work toward definite ends, and the influence of the superstructure upon its material base, were acknowledged by Engels in *Anti-Dühring* and in a letter to Joseph Bloch. It is also this ability of men to recognize the objective laws of natural and social development that caused the desertion of those aristocratic and bourgeois intellectuals from their respective classes.

And where is there a contradiction in the possibility of the natural and social worlds to solve problems and needs that arise? We are not dealing with static, inert entities, but with developing and vital phenomena. Does not the physical and the organic universe adapt to its environment? Does it not attempt to satisfy its needs? Is it not ingenious in its responses in the manner in which it makes up for a lack? And are these things not true in the human and social worlds as well? Is it not true that very often "Necessity is the mother of invention"? Like nature, society is an organic being which acts and lives in a fashion that transcends the will and the activities of each individual. When social problems and necessities arise they cannot be solved by an individual, who is not capable of grasping and understanding the entire social organism; social problems are solved, needs are met, inventions are produced, by the society as a whole with individuals each contributing his part to the total solution. For the society has a dynamic and a life of its own not dependent upon conscious individual cooperation.

Sartre has one last criticism to make of Marxist materialism, and with this criticism he aims at the very heart of Marxism's main claim to existence, i.e., its claim to be a socialist and therefore a humanist and a liberating philosophy. Because it is enamored with causality and causal determinism in the natural and social worlds, materialism makes an object out of man. Marxist theory asserts that it is able to chart man's actions and even his thoughts; it sees man as only a natural product, and in this way it decomposes him "into behavior patterns rigorously modelled upon Taylorist operations," and thus it "is playing into the master's hands."[20] It is a philosophy that betrays the human, which is the subjective in man. It sees him as a machine, a tool to be manipulated, to be exploited for its own ends, or for the ends of history. This is the first betrayal.

The second betrayal is materialism's promise to give man true freedom—economic, social, political. It promises an end to his alienation, which is the estrangement from his work, from the fruit of his labor, from his family, from society, from his species, and lastly even from his true self.[21] Marxism claims that this total alienation of man is the result of the capitalistic system which turns man and all his relations into commodity objects. In socialism it promises to give man back his freedom through a transformation of the economic structure of society. Yet where does Marxism find the means for such a transformation? Where can a materialistic, and therefore deterministic, theory unearth the elements such a transformation requires; is not man by nature an object and is not society by necessity a determined, rationally organized community? Where is there room for human freedom here? "A materialistic socialism is contradictory, therefore, because socialism establishes humanism as its end, a humanism which materialism renders inconceivable."[22] And a few pages later Sartre adds that a true revolutionary demands "the possibility for man to invent his own law. This is the basis of his humanism and of his socialism."[23] Materialism, in conformity to its basic principles, denies such a possibility to man, and so it deceives him by promising to bring him freedom, for its theory lends itself only to the promise of a regimented society.

But where, the Marxist asks, does Existentialism find the impudence to speak of humanism, particularly of humanism in a social context? Is it not Existentialism that maintains that all men are objects to each other and must forever remain so? And is it not Existentialism that adds that the only relation possible among human beings is conflict? Is this the Sartre who wrote "Hell is—other people,"[24] who now wants to speak of a social philosophy, of a socialistic humanism? And what of the freedom that

Existentialism promises to its converts; what does it provide for them? Nothing but a deep sense of anguish, abandonment, and perhaps bitterness and despair, for that is all the Existentialist freedom grants by its own admission. Existentialism, one of the most antisocial and egocentric philosophies ever to be developed by the mind of man, is not in any position to speak of humanism, socialism, and true human freedom. The humanism of Marx is one of a true community of men aiding each other in harmony toward progressive development in all spheres of social and personal life. And such work can proceed only if it is based upon realism, the real laws of natural and social development, and not upon a world of chaos, of absolute subjective interpretation, and a total *Nothingness*. Marxist socialism is a true operational humanism based upon the facts of reality. Marxism is therefore optimistic and hopeful in its work and in the results of its work. Existentialism can offer only a life steeped in pessimism and lonely despair, with no true social cooperation toward any useful purpose.

And so the polemical dialogue between Marxism and Existentialism concerning the question of materialism and its implications rests. It now becomes necessary to do some backtracking and to discuss a few of the main points raised during the debate.

First, as to the problem of God and any statements concerning his existence or non-existence. Actually both Marxism and Existentialism take *a priori* stands on the issue, and the Existentialist stand is even more abrupt than the Marxist. A Marxist at least attempts to give an explanation for his views, an explanation that may be challenged. The Existentialist, however, leaves no such background for challenge but simply declares that he has decided, for practical reasons, particularly his freedom, not to believe in God, or rather, to deny his existence. Sartre gives no real proofs of the non-existence of God, aside from the Anselmian argument in reverse: that the concept of one who is his own cause is self-contradictory. And that, says a commentator, "turns upon the elementary blunder of supposing that terms used of God are to be understood, not only in the sense in which they are used of man, but also in the sense in which they are used of man as he would be were there no God! One has the right to expect something better than that from a professional philosopher."[25] And one must expect something better, especially from a French Existentialist for whom the absence of God is one of the most important, if not the most important, prerequisite for the rest of his philosophy—the absence of human essence, of universal values, and the resulting absolute freedom and responsibility.

But in the end, the Existentialist would argue that whether in fact God does or does not exist makes little difference to him. As far as his personal life is concerned he may and does live it in a manner that requires no God. God is *not* a *reality-for-him,* and that is enough to say that there is no God. Existential atheism is therefore a personal atheism, and Existentialism does not argue the universal validity of atheism, only a personal validity. But since in Existentialism the only thing a person may be absolutely certain of is his own existence, even this personal validity becomes a matter of belief, which means, in other words, that it still remains an *a priori* stand. The fact that Existentialism does not deny that this is a metaphysical stand, does not absolve it of the *a priori* decision; and thereby its ability to criticize another view on the same question as an *a priori* stand is weakened, if not totally compromised. What saves the existential argument is materialism's claim that materialism does not take an *a priori* position on the issue, and in so far as Existentialism can demonstrate that materialism does indeed take such a position the argument is valid.

Several complications arise here. By arguing that the only thing any person is absolutely certain of is his own existence, and that "outside of the Cartesian *cogito* all objects are no more than probable."[26] Existentialism contradicts itself. For it first states that aside from "I exist" one cannot make a valid statement concerning anything else, and then it proceeds to apply this statement universally. It wants the impossible of eating its cake and having it too. If the only truth I know is the truth concerning my own existence, where do I obtain the right to claim that this also is the only truth that all other men know? By all logical rules I can speak only for myself, for I can never get outside of myself, and even more so, inside someone else. True, the "look" of others reveals to me their existence as "free" beings, but where does it follow that because they are free beings they too can be certain only of their existence and of nothing else? Even within the Existentialist philosophy it is not difficult to point out other facts that the individual is as certain of as his existence. Is he not absolutely certain of the existence of other beings like himself? It is the *cogito* itself that provides this certainty at the same time that it announces its existence. The "look" of the other beings reveals another certainty, that they are free beings. All these certainties are acceptable within the framework of the philosophy, but the extension to a universal rule of the subjective principle that the only absolute truth I know is the fact of my own existence is a contradiction.

But this is something of a digression from the matter of God's existence, to which it is now necessary to return. The classical positivist argument claims that any statements made concerning matters that lie outside of verifiable experience are metaphysical propositions and, as such, not given to truth or falsehood, but simply statements of nonsense. By this criterion it is true that both Marxists and Existentialists indulge in such metaphysical statements when they claim to be avowed atheists. In both cases it is a matter of belief. The only possible alternative seems to be agnosticism. But it can be validly argued that the decision not to make any statements about the matter is in itself an *a priori* attitude; however, this accusation would hold only if agnosticism were made into a universal dogma that maintained that no man was ever capable of making any valid statements about God. A confirmed agnostic of the universal type is in the same class as the confirmed theist and atheist. All three are making statements about matters which lie outside of their experience and which none of them can prove empirically.

One other problem remains under this topic: the definition of "experience." The concept of experience referred to above is a very narrow one indeed. It includes primarily experience of the material world. Yet there is an equally valid, and perhaps even more meaningful concept of experience applicable to men: the experience they have in the world of ethics, aesthetics, in personal relationships, and in perceiving the natural world *not* as a functional utilitarian reality, but as a fertile arena for the interaction of emotions. The experience in these areas is not given to the same empirical verification as is the experience of the material world, which is a phenomenon to be studied scientifically. And it is exactly in this scientifically unverifiable field of human emotional experiences that the concept of God plays the major role. If subjectivity exists in man's awareness of the physical world, an even greater subjectivity, in the sense of intangibility and different degrees of receptivity, exists in man's awareness of what could be called the emotional world.

Thus when the materialist states that experience has shown no God to exist, he is speaking only of the narrower aspects of experience; and because *his* "emotional" experience does not reveal to him any God, he cannot validly argue that the same is true of all other individual experiences. This last holds true for the Existentialist as well. The application of universally valid norms from one subjective experience is truly an *a priori* procedure, a procedure not warranted by logical and realistic thought. Therefore, contrary to what the materialist argues, there are certain forms of human experience which are subjective, and as such even uncommunicable; and contrary to what the Existentialist claims, these subjective experiences are not valid for all: they cannot be subjective and personal, and objective and universal at the same time.

An argument resembling to a large extent several of the problems treated above is that which concerns statements such as: all mind is matter; all matter is mind; all that is real is rational, and all that is rational is real. Once again these are statements transcending experience. Existentialism rightly claims that the materialist proposition, "all mind is matter" is the same in character as the idealist proposition, "all matter is mind." Logically they both belong to the same category, and both are unverifiable in experience simply because they are all-inclusive, while man's experience is finite. And similarly, therefore, both transcend experience and are metaphysical statements. Yet it must be admitted that a comparison of statements on a logical, theoretical, and abstract level may not always reveal the truths of reality. Mathematics and logic make many corresponding statements and categorize them, but do not claim for such categorization practical validity, only theoretical, analytic validity. The Existentialist argument has merit in pointing out to the materialist that he is making a statement concerning reality which is in the same class as the idealist's statement. But the materialist is correct in pointing to experience and to the practical world for the verification of his statement and for the rejection of the idealist one. The materialist could improve his argument by making his statement less universal, i.e., provisional: *so far* experience has proved that all mind arises from matter; let the idealist prove the opposite. He could make the same request concerning God. However, Marxist materialism makes no such reservations, and in this lies its mistake and its fall into metaphysics, as Sartre rightly maintains. At the same time, Existentialism does not fare any better with its subjective yet universally applicable statements.

This same fall into metaphysics is true of the materialist doctrine that the world is rational. First, what does this mean—rational? That all things operate according to certain predictable laws? That all things are capable of being understood by the mind of man? Or that all things in the universe are caused, that they are what they are, and do what they do, because of some prior cause, which again can be found and understood by man? And that, therefore, all things can be explained sooner or later, or at least that such a possibility exists, although it may not be humanly possible to accomplish? The materialist answer to all these questions is in the affirmative: this is what is meant by the statement that the world is rational. But how can one be certain of any of these hypotheses without again forming *a priori* conclusions? Yet materialism is certain. But if it is certain of the universality of these "rational" laws, what does it do with physical and organic accidents (earthquakes, floods, collision of stars, freaks) which defy the rational laws of nature? Certainly exceptions do not prove the rule. If the world is rational, then the accidents, too, must have a cause which can be discovered. If this is so, then these accidents must have their own laws—perhaps perverse laws and not as rational as the rest of nature, but still laws. But who is to decide what is an exception, an accident, and what is the rule? And what happens to the theory that all things are rational? A contradiction arises: all things are rational and even those things which are not rational are rational. A contradiction and a tautology. And in the process the words "law" and "rational" have lost all meaning. And yet the materialists continue to make such statements as the following: "The world is matter moving in conformity to law, and our knowledge, being the highest product of nature, is in a position only to *reflect* this conformity to law."[27] In the

light of the above problems concerning a rational definition of law, the statement is meaningless, unless it means
that our mind *reflects* all things that happen in the universe, laws and any absence of laws.

This brings us to the point maintained by the Existentialists that the world as it comes to the mind of the individual is simply a disorganized, chaotic mess to which man
must give order.[28] In this respect, the Existentialist does
not deny the validity of science, but he thinks that its facts
are not conclusive but are subject to different kinds of interpretations, none of which can be absolutely verified.
Such a view opens the door wide to rampant skepticism
and is at the same time just as dogmatic as the view that
the facts of science are objectively true and not given to
individual subjective interpretation. The problem continuously appears that any statement of a general character
applied to any aspect of existence tends to be absolute and
a priori. The total agnosticism of Hume is a tempting escape out of the predicament, but that, too, if applied universally, meets with the same problem. There is no doubt
that the materialistic emphasis upon *practice*, upon *acting*
in life, is the only realistic possibility of overcoming all
such philosophical riddles. This same emphasis on practice
and acting is also a necessity for the Existentialist, since
he can verify his own existence and create his own essence
only in relation to and in interaction with the practical
world of daily life. However, the materialist drives the
criterion of practice to an extreme when he demands that
it serve as the *only* criterion for *all* truth. It serves well in
the material world, but again in the realms of art, music,
and other human emotional activities, the criterion of practice as a principle for the verification of truth is almost
useless. How does it apply here at all? And again it is in
this sphere that the matter of God falls. Also, these subjective aspects of human experience should not be relegated
to a minor place in man's total life; on the contrary, they
form the major, if not the only significant, part of his ex-

istence. His interaction with the material world is important, and here practice is his teacher, but even while he acts upon the material world, his emotional functions also play an important role, to the extent that even the known rules of practice may be disregarded to his material or physical detriment.

Turning once again to science, a focal point of the argument between materialism and Existentialism in this respect is the matter of causation. An interesting confrontation of the two opposed views is found in a discussion following Sartre's presentation of his essay, "Existentialism and Humanism" (first published in 1946 and known as the most popular presentation of Sartre's form of Existentialism). Sartre's interlocutor is the known French Marxist Naville:

M. Naville

. . . For us, a situation is a totality that is constructed, and that reveals itself, by a whole series of determining factors, and these determinants are causal, including causality of a statistical kind.

M. Sartre

You talk to me about causality of a statistical order. That is meaningless. Will you tell me, precisely and clearly, what you understand by causality? I will believe in the Marxian causality upon the very day when a Marxist explains it to me. Whenever anyone speaks to you of freedom you spend your time saying, "Excuse me, but there is causality." But of this secret causality, which has no meaning except in Hegel, you can render no account. You have a dream about the Marxian causality.

M. Naville

Do you admit the existence of scientific truth? There may be spheres in which no kind of truth is predictable. But the world of objects—this you will nevertheless admit, I hope—is the world with which the sciences are concerned. Yet for you, this is a world in which there are only probabilities, never amounting to the truth. The world of objects, then, which is that of science, admits of no absolute truth. But it does attain to relative truth. Now, you will admit that the sciences employ the notion of causality?

M. Sartre

Certainly not. The sciences are abstract; they study the variations of factors that are equally abstract, and not real causality. We are concerned with universal factors upon a plane where their relations can always be studied: whereas, in Marxism, one is engaged in the study of a single totality, in which one searches for causality. But it is not at all the same thing as scientific causality.[29]

It is evident that the two men speak of different matters when they use the word causality. Sartre admits to the notion of causality only as an abstract formula; whereas Naville sees causality as an objective fact of the world, which man recognizes and perhaps utilizes. In this difference lies their disagreement. In reality, both are pursuing their views of causality to an absurd extreme, yet neither will yield a step because for each the conception of causality that he holds is a logical necessity in his philosophy; without it the rest of the system would not hold together. Marxist materialism would have to eliminate its ideas of the socially caused human conscience, the materially determined human existence, and the economically produced superstructure, as well as the inevitable triumph of socialism. Existentialism would have to give up its idea of total human freedom. If such retreats were made the philosophies would have to end their existence as distinct philosophical systems; it is no surprise, therefore, that Naville and Sartre hold so tenaciously to their particular definitions of causality.

There remains one last major problem mentioned in the foregoing debate between Marxism and Existentialism which should be discussed in greater detail. It is the Marxist contention that ideas and men arise out of the social situation when that situation is in need of them. Even before discussing the qualification of this statement made by the Marxists themselves, the issue arises as to what a "need" is. There is a temptation to apply *post hoc ergo propter hoc* reasoning: all that comes into being comes into being because it is needed. This leaves one with the self-satisfying Hegelian notion that all that exists is necessary and therefore reasonable and good. Clearly such reasoning is an assumption that ends all further discussion. But ignoring for the moment this unpromising conclusion, particularly for academic study, the question must be asked as to who is to decide what is needed and what is not needed in a particular society at a particular time. And what happens when there is a need but the idea or the man does not appear? For example, the socialist movement in Germany in the decade after the First World War needed a man of Lenin's caliber to organize the various socialist groups and to lead them to a victorious socialist revolution. Germany was certainly ripe for such a revolution at that time; all that it lacked was the leader. And he never came. Numerous other such examples can be found in history when a nation needed a man for a specific task, but he never appeared, and the nation suffered as a result. The same is true of ideas and inventions. To argue that a man or an idea did not appear when needed because he or it was not *really* needed ends with the above concept of Hegel and again brings all discussion to a close.

There is also a contradiction involved in this Marxist theory, a contradiction mentioned before at the end of the first chapter and posed by Sartre as well: If all men and ideas are the direct products of their social environ-

ment, how is it possible for them to divorce themselves
from their environment and act upon it, and, more im-
portantly, against it? Marxism itself agrees that at times
men and ideas arise ahead of their time, before the situation is ripe for them. How is such an occurrence possible?
One of Marx's favorite heroes in history was Spartacus.
But Spartacus is a problem for Marxist theory. His revolt,
Marxists say, had to fail, for the ideas he was propagating
were at least two thousand years ahead of their time. But
how did they arise in the first place? Why was it that a
slave reared and educated in a society in which slavery
was an approved social feature, and which relied upon
slaves as an economic necessity should revolt against his
environment? The Existentialist, of course, has a ready
answer: at all times, in all places, man by his nature is a
free being. But the Marxist is hard-pressed for an explanation, because slaves revolting, especially at a time when
no such revolt was called for by the historical or the economic conditions, certainly do not "reflect" the social environment. Perhaps the Existentialist has a point; Marxism
has studied man from only one aspect—his socio-economic
life—and has ignored an equally important part of his being—his psychological makeup. It has studied man as if
his entire psychology were determined by the socio-economic forces, and it has ignored the possibility that his
organism may have powers over which such forces do not
have a determining effect.

Once more, if society takes up only the problems that
it is already capable of solving,[30] why do unsoluble problems exist? Existentialism points to several of these: the
problems of morality, values, freedom, and even the
problem of the purpose of life itself. The Polish Marxist
philosopher, Adam Schaff, acknowledges this debt to Existentialism, particularly on the issue of a situation with
conflicting moral norms and the resulting need of a
choice not determined by any norms: "Existentialism is
to be commended for having raised the theoretical ques-

tion, although it has not been in a position to solve it. Potentially, Marxism is best equipped to solve it; but so far this has been only a possibility."[31] True, and the question even today remains unanswered; no solutions seem to be forthcoming out of the material means of production. And according to a strict interpretation of the theory these problems should never have come to light in the first place.

It is the same glaring contradiction in Marxism that keeps coming back again and again: men, ideas, society are determined by operative physical, economic, and social causes, and yet they can be free of all these causes at times, if not always. Which is it? It cannot be both together. Marxism holds on to both, for it needs the determinism and it needs causation; but to be realistic as well as revolutionary, it is forced to explain and even to rely upon situations as if determinism and causation did not apply. Thus it must sustain the contradiction within itself for the sake of its existence as a theory.

chapter three

THE DIALECTIC

If materialism is the foundation of Marxism, then certainly the dialectic is the movement that gives life to this foundation and so makes Marxism an operational theory. The entire universe, as described by Hegel, develops in conformity with a dialectical process, i.e., a thesis exists that out of necessity, it seems, must give rise to its antitheses, and, again through a necessary interplay between these two, a synthesis is formed, incorporating supposedly the superior elements of both the thesis and the antithesis; the synthesis itself in turn becomes a thesis, and the process continues indefinitely forward. It is in this fashion that the *Weltgeist* progressively crystallizes itself in the universe until it is perfectly superimposed upon the universe, and the two become one.

It has become a commonplace, thanks to Marx, that "the dialectic of Hegel was placed upon its head; or rather, turned off its head, on which it was standing and placed upon its feet."[1] And instead of being the development of an Absolute Spirit, it "reduced itself to the science of the general laws of motion, both of the external world and of human thought. . . ."[2]

It is exactly in this reversal that Sartre commences his criticism of the dialectic as it is applied in Marxism. He admits that the dialectic is true in ideas, for ideas are by nature synthetic, producing a unity which encompasses all parts previously given; also the parts are inseparably interrelated, producing a homogeneous totality: a part could not be examined if isolated or separated from the

whole without being distorted. It is because of this nature of ideas that Hegel is justified in using the dialectic,
for in his philosophy the universe is an "idea." However,
once Marx has performed his "Copernican Revolution" and
substituted matter for the Hegelian Spirit, then the justification for the use of the dialectic as a description of the
world and its processes is rescinded. For matter is not
synthetic but analytic; it can be broken down into its
constituent parts without those parts undergoing any
changes as a result of their separation. Furthermore, the
dialectic is characterized by internal movement, whereas
matter is inert and receives all movement from without.
Matter is quantitative and isolated; the dialectic is qualitative and interrelated. It is not Hegel who errs, as Marx
claims, in his application of the dialectic, it is Marx himself who is at fault.[3] His reversal of the dialectic is not
warranted by the facts, especially by the facts of science
on which Marxism so heavily relies for documenting the
validity of the dialectic movement in material nature.

Sartre finds that science, in its principles and methods,
is the opposite of dialectical. In science all things are
reducible to quantitative units. True, science sometimes
uses the word "syntheses," but never in the Hegelian
sense, because the particles forming a combination retain
their properties. "If an atom of oxygen combines with
atoms of sulphur and hydrogen to form acid, it retains
its identity. Neither water nor acid is a real whole which
changes and governs its composing elements, but simply
a passive resultant, a *state*."[4] And Sartre adds that in all
of science we never encounter an organic totality.

He also castigates Engels for speaking of "natural history" when the latter utilized Darwin to help buttress the
dialectic as a natural fact. History can only be human,
since it is a "deliberate resumption of the past by the
present";[5] Darwin demonstrated not a history of nature
but a hypothesis that nature proceeds in its development
by a series of mechanical, quantitative changes. The

struggle for existence, for example, does not produce a new dialectical synthesis through a fusion of opposites, but, on the contrary, simply eliminates the weaker elements.

Again, contrary to the claims of Engels, changes in physics are not from quantity to quality, but only a continuation of quantitative effects. The famous "qualitative" transformation of water to ice or steam is not a change in quality but a result of a change in quantity: the quantitative progression of temperature which is measurable in units. This is how science sees the matter; it is only the naïve perception of man that treats the change as a qualitative one, for he feels temperature as a quality and sees the changes it produces as changes of quality. But a scientist substitutes a quantitative measurement for the vague feelings of the senses: "We must therefore choose. Either we remain within the domain of perceptible quality, in which case steam is a quality and so is temperature; we are not being scientific; we witness the action of one quality on another. Or else we regard temperature as a quantity."[6] And even if, for the sake of argument, it is allowed that the change of water to steam is a qualitative change, there is no dialectical progression: water changes to steam and eventually steam changes back to water. It is a cycle and not a progression.

Contrary to the characteristics of dialectical relations, which are internal and qualitative, science always remains with relations which are quantitative and external. It does not study the concrete and particular reality and events, but studies the abstract and general conditions of the universe. The Hegelian dialectic, therefore, proceeds by synthesizing and by moving from the abstract (idea) to the concrete (world), whereas the movement of science is the opposite: it proceeds by analyzing and by moving from the concrete (event) to the abstract (law). And when looking at modern life and reality, if all these ar-

guments are carried to their conclusions, the result is
that;

> . . . the bourgeoisie, is materialist; its method of
> thinking is analysis, and its ideology is science. . . .
> the proletariat, is idealist; its method of thinking is
> synthesis, and its ideology is dialectic. And as there
> is a struggle between the classes, the ideologies
> should be incompatible. But this is not the case. It
> seems that the dialectic is the crown of science and
> makes full use of its results. It seems that the bour-
> geoisie, availing itself of analysis and then reducing
> the higher to the lower, is idealist, whereas the pro-
> letariat—which thinks synthetically and is guided by
> the revolutionary idea—even when affirming the irre-
> ducibility of a synthesis to its elements, is materialist.
> What are we to make of this?[7]

It appears, therefore, that Marxism attempts to reconcile two contradictory concepts—science and the dialectic.
Thus it claims at one time that life is only a complex
physico-chemical process, and at another time that it is
an irreducible moment in the dialectic of nature. At one
time it claims that mechanical determinism is obsolete
and has been replaced by the dialectic, and at another
time it reverts to an explanation of concrete situations
by causal, external principles. "One feels throughout their
confused discourse," writes Sartre, "that they have in-
vented the slippery and contradictory notion of reducible
irreducibles."[8]

But there are other problems that arise if the dialectic
is fused with materialism. In Hegel the *Weltgeist* is not
fully given at the beginning but has to develop and crys-
tallize with history; the dialectic and history progress in
unison. But if matter replaces the *Weltgeist*, it is already
fully present since all of it is given in the universe; the
dialectic no longer generates the world or moves it progressively: reality—nature, man, society—only reflects a

part of an already fully established dialectical universe. But if the dialectic no longer functions as a progressive generator, constantly enriching the world with new contents, then it does nothing, and it is no longer the dialectic. This annihilation of the dialectic by Marxists is possible only because they adhere to a contradictory notion of matter: "At times it is the poorest of abstractions and at others the richest of concrete totalities, depending on their needs."[9]

Another problem is how did the dialectic succeed in retaining its necessity during the change from Spirit to matter? In Hegel necessity was part of the dialectic, and there was a "progressive identification of the dialectic of consciousness with the consciousness of the dialectic."[10] But now, if the dialectic *represents* the manner in which the material world develops, and if the development of consciousness is no longer identified with the development of the dialectic but is simply a partial reflection of reality, and if it is influenced by feelings and ideologies that do not have their origin in the consciousness, then again the dialectic is nothing, for its necessity no longer holds. At best it has an effect here and there, and then moves on. Nevertheless, Marxist theory retains the necessity and the certainty of the dialectical development, even though necessity and certainty are applicable only to Hegel's *Weltgeist* and not to the material universe. In the insistence upon a synthetic, dialectic, certain, and necessary development of matter, Marxism has turned matter into an idea. It has slid into idealism. And so Sartre concludes: "Just as the Marxists claim to be positivists and destroy their positivism through the use they implicitly make of metaphysics, just as they proclaim their rationalism and destroy it by their conception of the origin of thought, so, at the very moment they posit it, they deny their basic principle, materialism, by a furtive recourse to idealism."[11] Thus all that the dialectic has done for Marxian materialism is to have destroyed it by achieving the opposite effect of placing Marxism in the idealistic camp.

As usual, Sartre presents strong arguments for his beliefs. But let us observe what happens to the arguments when they are examined with some care or opposed by other arguments. First, how true is it that only ideas are synthetic and nature is not; and second, how true is it that the material universe contains no organic totalities whose parts if analyzed would remain undisturbed through the process of separation?

Sartre admits the soundness of the dialectic if applied to ideas; yet for ideas to be true they must reflect the objective world. If there were no synthesis in the objective world then synthetic ideas would remain abstract and unreal representations of the world in the manner of metaphysical ideas. If ideas are synthetic and if they correctly represent or interpret the nature of reality, then it is because reality is synthetic. And science, as it will be shown below, has proved that reality is indeed synthetic. And Sartre does admit that science "has at least proved itself."[12]

Granting the above, all that Marxism claims is that to understand reality as it really is one must examine it as it really is; and since reality is dialectical one must think dialectically if a true knowledge of the world is desired: "An exact representation of the universe, of its evolution, of the development of mankind, and of the reflection of this evolution in the minds of men, can therefore only be obtained by the methods of dialectics, with its constant regard to the innumerable actions and reactions of life and death, of progressive or retrogressive changes."[13] However, Sartre seems not to want to admit that the universe is dialectical, that it is not static but continuously in development through its own internal motion. Also, he does not think that organic phenomena are synthetic in nature. For example, the close synthetic (in the manner of ideas) interconnection of the parts which make up the human brain is a fact that he ignores. Yet how is it possible to separate the various parts of the brain without doing damage to those parts and to all other parts, for the entire function of the brain and its products, including the most important product—consciousness—is dependent upon the organic totality and synthetic union of its parts? The same is equally true of a cell of protoplasm or a cell of chlorophyll. But all this does not mean that a synthesis cannot be analyzed and reduced to its parts; it is not true as Sartre claims that "according to the very idea of synthesis, life cannot be reduced to matter and human consciousness cannot be reduced to life."[14] Sartre's difficulty is that by his rejection of dialectics, and therefore of one of its laws, the transformation of quantity to quality, he cannot envision such a reduction. Yet this is exactly what science attempts to accomplish when it analyzes the components of a cell of chlorophyll or protoplasm; and when it succeeds in reuniting them and producing a live cell it will be but one more witness to this law of the change of quantity to quality.

But all these objections of Sartre's are related to his objections to causation as a fact of nature (Chapter Two); by his own admission, the universe is simply a viscous, opaque mass without reason or order. Any reason or laws found in the universe are only abstract, manmade hypotheses removed from objective reality. But Sartre contradicts himself when he states that science has proved itself—what does this mean but that science gives a true representation of the world?—and at the same time claims that the universe is a chaotic mass of matter without any rhyme or reason. Science has shown the opposite to be true; let Sartre demonstrate that its laws and findings are false in their interpretations of the universe. And if the universe is in chaos, is not chaos an order of sorts—the lack of order—which acts according to its own chaotic laws? Besides, what criteria of order does Sartre use in announcing that the universe is in disorder?

Sartre does not bother to disprove the claims of science but simply makes undemonstrated assertions of the above nature. The same is true of the argument that in opposition to the internal movement of the dialectic, the movement of matter comes from without and is external. What does Sartre mean by stating that matter is inert, that movement and energy come from outside of it? If he admits that the universe is material, whence does all movement and energy proceed if not from matter itself? As for the inertness of matter, it would be best first to examine Sartre's views in greater detail. He writes: "Now the fact is that matter is characterized by its inertia. This means that it is incapable of producing anything by itself. It is a *vehicle* of movements and of energy, and it always receives these movements and this energy from without. It borrows them and relinquishes them."[15] (Italics added.) And in another place he adds in a note: "And let us not forget, moreover, that a body always receives its energy from without (even intra-atomic energy is so received); it is within the framework of the general principle of inertia that we are able to study the problem of equivalence of energy. To make energy the vehicle of the dialectic would be to transform it by violence into *idea*."[16]

Apparently Sartre does not agree with the scientific definition of an atom as the "ground state of energy," with the energy remaining in the atom even at the hypothetical absolute zero point where all movement stops. In the same footnote, partially quoted above, he argues that energy (like causation and the dialectic) is only a concept of convenience fashioned by science in order to account for certain phenomena. This last is obviously true since all representations of the universe and of its activities can be expressed only as concepts; the point is to demonstrate that the concepts are false or do not sufficiently express the universe as it really is.

Also it is a true fact, again contrary to Sartre's un-

proved statements, that the atom's movement comes from
within. The atom is not inert; on the contrary, it is the
basic state of energy. And if physical matter is not inert,
certainly organic matter is far from inert; if physical matter obtains its energy from within, certainly organic matter is basically directed from within.

Again, it is contrary to scientific facts to assert, as
Sartre does, that the union of different atoms, as, for example, sulphur, oxygen, and hydrogen, produces a combination in which the atoms retain their identity and remain unchanged in their composition. Under very special
conditions it is possible to obtain the following reaction:
a union of hydrogen, sulphur, and oxygen giving sulphuric
acid. However, in the synthesis the atoms forming the
combination do *not* retain their structure or, especially,
their properties.

In his argument Sartre does not state whether he is
speaking of microscopic or macroscopic properties. His
claim has some validity as far as the microscopic structure
of the atoms and their combination is concerned; however,
even here the matter is not exactly as he would like to
have it. For the atom, as a material particle, is described
by its structure and by its weight function, and both of
these undergo changes when the atom combines with
other atoms. The valid part of Sartre's argument is that
the nuclei of, say, hydrogen, sulphur, and oxygen remain
undisturbed and are identifiable in the combination; this
is not true of the electrons, which in the combination no
longer retain their former positions but mix freely with the
electrons of the other atoms, producing a totally different
electron grouping. But if Sartre is speaking of the
macroscopic properties of atoms, then his statement that
the "particles forming a combination retain their properties"[17] is false. Hydrogen and oxygen are gases at room
temperature and sulphur is a solid, but sulphuric acid,
among its other characteristics, exists only as a water solution and is highly corrosive—both properties not found in

the elements that form it when they are in a separate state.

The above may seem a quibble, yet it is a necessary one because it and the other arguments presented clearly demonstrate that there is no radical separation between the principles of dialectics and the natural world. Both are synthetic, qualitative (as well as quantitative), and moved from within; matter is not characterized only by its inertness, quantitativeness, and isolation, as Sartre maintains. He simply distorts or ignores facts; thus, for example, his argument that the struggle for existence is quantitative, with a pure mechanical elimination of the weaker elements, ignores the fact that definite qualitative changes do take place as organisms progress, and that the elimination of weaker elements is likewise a trait of the dialectic. This scientifically established progress of organic life, which by all known facts has its origin in matter, similarly runs contrary to the Existentialist's argument that matter, unlike the dialectic, cannot generate the world and add to it new progressive contents.

Before examining Sartre's other claim, that nature cannot have a history, it would once more be best to begin by a more detailed description of his proposition. He quotes Engels as having written that, "in the last analysis, Nature proceeds dialectically, that it does not move in an eternally identical circle that perpetually repeats itself, but that it has a real history."[18] Evidently the words are from *Socialism: Utopian and Scientific,* which was first published in French. The English translation by Edward Aveling, Marx's son-in-law, gives the last phrase of that statement as follows: "but goes through a real historical evolution."[19] There is some difference between nature having a "real history" and going through a "real historical evolution." Certainly the latter is in the spirit of the intended meaning, particularly since, as Sartre correctly points out, Engels then proceeds to mention Darwin as a support for his thesis. But this is truly a minor quibble, and its resolution either way would have little influence upon the fact that *all* things have a history—the cosmos, the earth, nature, and man. If one restricts the concept of history, as Sartre does, to a "deliberate resumption of the past by the present,"[20] then history is almost non-existent, i.e., if by "deliberate" is meant conscious or self-conscious, for even man and societies resume their past not deliberately but mainly unconsciously. Besides, the past does not have to be resumed deliberately; it is already there as a given, immediately providing the situation and having an influence upon the present.

It is possible that Sartre wishes to emphasize the fact that man's deliberate attitude toward history, whether of acceptance or rejection, makes a difference in his behavior. This would be a true argument in respect to social history, for a person may know the laws of historical movement and still act contrary to them: for example, refusing to accept the development of society to new forms as good or advantageous, and hindering this development and in this way changing the development and the laws, even if to a minor extent. But the argument is not valid in respect to natural history, where the acceptance or the rejection of natural facts and laws has no influence upon these facts or laws, even though it may have an influence upon the behavior of the person involved.

The entire problem of social and natural history arises here mainly because of Existentialism's conception of history, or, more correctly, because of its conception of man and the world. Since the material world is in a state of chaos, no discernible history is possible, for history implies the examination of one spatio-temporal fact through its process of change and evolution in time. Such an examination cannot be carried out if all is in chaos and there is no visible order. In regard to the history of man, the problem is of a slightly different nature. Because each man at basis is a nothingness, it means that he is absolutely free and by his own decisions forms his essence; in other words, he makes his history, or, rather, he decides by himself which parts of the past—his and mankind's—he wishes to acknowledge and accept as his own. In this sense, then, history is a *deliberate* acceptance of the past by the present. And because nature is not characterized by the freedom of man it cannot resume its past deliberately; therefore only human history is possible.

Now these are very strange attitudes toward history, and they again contradict all that science has demonstrated and achieved. The question to be answered is whether Sartre admits that the world existed before there was a man to perceive it and deliberately to assume its present and its past. If he wishes to avoid the open solipsism and idealism of Berkeley, then he must agree that the world is not dependent in its existence upon man's perception of it: it is there, perceived or not. And if he admits this, then he must also admit that the world has its own history, regardless of man's recognition or denial of this fact. Again science is clear on this issue and demonstrates by its investigations in geology and biology that the earth existed long before man came on the scene. Sartre accuses Marxism of attempting to reconcile two opposed concepts—science and the dialectic, but it is rather he who attempts a reconciliation of contradictory ideas—science and Existentialism.

Next, Sartre misunderstands what is meant by quantity and quality; he insists that the transformation of water to ice or steam is only a quantitative change, the result of a quantitative addition of temperature. But Marxists agree that it is the addition of quantity which produces the change in the water; Sartre, however, seems not to grant that the water has changed with the quantitative additions, that it has properties as steam or ice which water did not have, "that the properties of steam are not simply the properties of hot water increased in degree. The water has become something that is no longer water."[21] This does not mean that the new qualitative state has no relation at all to the old qualities. However, the change is not a gradual one: "We cannot find a little bit of ice in water before it reaches the freezing point. We find no ice at all. An acorn is not a small oak tree which grows larger merely by quantitative increase of existing properties. The acorn does not have a small trunk, tiny branches and microscopic leaves. These things are totally absent until a new level of development is reached."[22] And then the transformation is one of a change in quality. It is according to this dialectic that all nature progresses. Sartre sees a cycle and not a progression in the change of water to ice or steam; he would argue in a similar manner for the acorn and the tree. But evolution is a slow and almost imperceptible movement lasting millions of years; the acorn and its tree which seem to be engaged in only a cyclical process have not always been what they are today, but have evolved from a more primitive growth. Reproduction is in most cases cyclical; however, even in the apparent cycle, unperceived changes constantly occur, and with time they do become visible. Even though man's reproduction appears cyclical, there is little doubt that he has evolved from other species and is still in a process of evolution to a different species in the future: the process is to human eyes almost non-existent, and it may even escape science, but it is still there as the past has definitely shown.

Therefore, once more, there is no contradiction in maintaining that life is a complex of physico-chemical processes and at the same time in dialectical development. Science does not study, as Sartre indicates, the abstract and the general conditions of the universe; it abstracts and formulates general laws from the real, concrete, and particular events that it examines. It both analyzes and synthesizes.

Sartre's final argument against the dialectic is that in Marxism the dialectic cannot retain several of the traits which it had in Hegel's philosophy—necessity, the power of generation, and the progressive development ending in man's consciousness of its laws and reality. Sartre fails to recognize that in its rejection of Hegel's idealism Marxism also rejected any absolute certainty and necessity in respect to the dialectic and its laws. This does not, however, invalidate the facts that science has uncovered which indicate that nature does indeed act in a dialectical fashion, that the universe is generated by dialectical principles. And as in Hegel, it is still true that it develops progressively, and that man, the highest being that it has produced, is able to come to a conscious understanding of the laws that are responsible for his development.

Sartre writes in one place that the dialectic may be regarded "as a working hypothesis, as a method to be tried, a method which is justified if proved successful."[23] It is his contention that Marxists do not view dialectics in this manner but regard it as an absolute and a necessary law of natural movement and development. Yet a commentator on Marxism speaks of the dialectical laws in the following manner:

> The position taken is that all that has been found [objective scientific evidence] supports them and nothing that has been found invalidates them. While in their generalized form we may thus accept them as proved principles, we can by no means settle the question of their concrete application to particular fields simply by means of deduction. The evidence so far accumulated in their favor should lead us to employ them as the principle hypotheses or tools in the investigation of further areas of subject matter. "Not a single principle of dialectics" we are told in an authoritative source [*Bolshaia Sovetskaia Entsiklopedia*], "can be converted into an abstract schema from which, by purely logical means, it would be

possible to infer the answer to concrete questions. These principles are a guide to activity and scientific research, not a dogma."[24]

The conflicts between Marxism and Existentialism concerning the dialectic are thus exhausted, but the arguments continue and may be reviewed further from a nonpartisan point of view. The dialectic is truly a phenomenon difficult to define. Its laws—movement, development, transformation, in short, change—are so general that they are able to engulf almost everything; and, as the argument runs, everything is nothing, for it is no longer distinct and definable. If the dialectic simply meant that nothing in the universe is static but everything is in a process of change, this could be accepted as a very broad but realistic hypothesis, not an absolute principle. But the Marxists assign to the dialectic a greater function than simply stating that all is change. The dialectic somehow seems to regulate this change according to recognizable or rational principles; what is more, it regulates the changes not to a retrogressive or a cyclical but to a progressive end. (Progress seems to be defined by greater complexity and specialization of functions.) Furthermore the dialectic is applicable not only to the physical universe but to society as well, to social development, and, from this, to art, ethics, and, of course, thought. Once again it is an all-encompassing principle. There are dialectical laws that guide history: the changes in the forces of production; dialectical laws that guide social development: the struggle of classes; dialectical laws that guide thought by a reflection of the dialectical laws of nature: The Law of Strife, Interpenetration and Unity of Opposites, the Law of Transformation of Quantity into Quality and vice versa, and the Law of the Negation of the Negation.

If one wishes to multiply laws it is not a difficult task to perform. There is a law for walking: standing upright and using one's legs for locomotion; a law for crossing the street without being hit by a vehicle: making one's way across the street when no vehicles are in sight; a law for maximizing profits: selling more and more products at a price higher than their cost, etc. Since all these laws are laws of movement, why not call them dialectical? And since each one of these laws may be interpreted as a qualitative negation of a former state, why not call the principle of the Negation of the Negation into operation? This is, of course, carrying dialectic to absurdity; but unless Marxists propose more definable criteria for what is dialectical and what is not, unless they state clearly what their hypothesis is, they have little to say when the dialectic is pulled to such extremes.

Sartre is also justified in arguing that Marxism in its general intonations speaks of dialectics as an absolute and objectively real principle and not a hypothesis, as was the case with causation. A strong implication of necessity and determinism does exist in Marxist interpretations of the world, a necessity and a determinism deduced from causation and dialectics as absolute truths. Sartre is equally correct in arguing that when these are not tenable, Marxists often shift to interpretations not warranted by their theories, and thus they hold contradictory notions. However, Sartre with his Existentialism takes the other extreme of absolute anarchy and chaos and so maintains theories of the world which are realistically (scientifically) untenable; his weaknesses have been adequately revealed in the Marxist replies to his arguments.

chapter four

THE REVOLUTION

"The philosophers have only *interpreted* the world, in various ways; the point, however, is to *change* it."[1] Marxists have guided themselves by these words of their founder to the present day. But *changing* and *interpreting* the world are movements not necessarily related or tied to each other. It is possible, for example, to hold a theory of a socialist revolution, with the proletariat as the agent of the revolution, and even with a belief in the inevitable triumph of the revolution, without necessarily at the same time holding a materialistic interpretation of the universe. Marxists would object to such a separation, for their philosophy seems to be closely dependent upon materialism as an explanation of revolutionary possibilities. But it only "seems"; in fact, the division is a possibility which would not damage either side—revolution or materialism. The belief in the reality of such a separation is also the view of Sartre; he, however, regards the split as a necessity if Marxism wishes to remain a revolutionary philosophy. Materialism, he claims, is pernicious for a theory of revolution.

In the second part of his essay, "Materialism and Revolution," Sartre attempts to demonstrate the pitfalls for a revolutionary philosophy which is attached too closely to materialism. First, he defines the makings of a revolutionary and his situation; then he proceeds to develop a philosophy of revolution that would satisfy the revolutionary's theoretical and practical needs; and throughout the discussion he shows where materialism fails to meet those needs. The paragraphs below will provide a summary of the main points of his argument, and the possible Marxist view of the matter will follow each major division.

The Revolutionary

A revolution, according to Sartre's understanding, takes place when a change of social institutions is accompanied by a profound alteration in the property system. The revolutionary is one who acts intentionally to produce such a change. He becomes a revolutionary because he is in a situation in which he feels oppressed, and he finds that the only realistic remedy for his state is revolution. Not all who are oppressed are revolutionaries; e.g., Negroes in the United States, Jews, and others, are not revolutionaries because they simply wish to be integrated into their societies, to share in the same privileges as its other members: they seek no modification of the property system, at least not directly. A revolutionary, on the other hand, finds himself in an oppressed situation from which his escape can be effected only by a change in the social institutions and the property relations which oppress him; for it is exactly as an oppressed person that he is indispensable to the society. Such an oppressed person who is indispensable to society is the worker, "and it is as a worker that he is oppressed."[2] This defines the revolutionary situation, but not as yet the revolutionary, for the worker may not question the property rights of the entrepreneur but simply strive for better working conditions and wages. He becomes a revolutionary only when he attempts a total break with the present social and property institutions and acts to bring about a better future. Because he knows that he cannot bring about his liberation as an individual, since as a member of the working class he can never become integrated with the privileged classes, he therefore acts for the liberation of the entire oppressed working class. And he hopes that in the lib-

erated society "the relationships of solidarity which he
maintains with other workers will become the very model
of human relationships."[3]

It becomes imperative at this stage to mention Sartre's
conceptions of the origins of classes and class-consciousness which are developed in some of his more theoretical
writings, particularly in *Being and Nothingness*. For in
"Materialism and Revolution" the picture he paints of the
unity and solidarity of the revolutionary working class is at
some variance with his existential ontology. It is also necessary to describe his differences with Marxism in this
important area of class and class-consciousness.

Sartre would agree with Marx that social classes do exist, that some of them are a product of the economic
system, that human nature is related to class membership,
and that ideology is a result of the class struggle.[4] Nevertheless, the remaining differences between their conceptions of class almost obliterate any agreement. Existentialism, by its ontology, demands that there be constant
conflict among each and every individual regardless of the
class to which the individual may belong. This means that
even though a conflict exists among classes, a conflict of
perhaps equal importance exists at the same time among
the individual members of every class. The solidarity and
homogeneity of a class are thus broken; also, conflict is
extended to the future classless society. Class conflict, Sartre would hold, results from the needs of the underprivi-
leged classes to change the existing situation; it is conditioned by economic factors but not determined by them,
as in Marxism. Class conflict and class consciousness are
primarily subjective movements. The subjectivity arises
as a result of Sartre's definition of class consciousness and
class unity as products of the "looks" of the members of
the privileged classes:

> The primary fact is that the member of the oppressed
> collectivity, who as a simple person is engaged in

fundamental conflicts with other members of this
collectivity (love, hate, rivalry of interests, etc.),
apprehends his condition and that of other members
of this collectivity as *looked-at and thought about
by consciousnesses which escape him.*[5] (Italics
added.)

The social and economic organization in a capitalistic
society which provides honor and privileges for the bourgeois aids the development of class-consciousness and class
unity in the workers because the bourgeois look at the
workers as "objects"—as things to be utilized for the benefit of the bourgeoisie. At the same time the bourgeoisie
does not feel itself to be a class because when the workers
look at its members they see them as "subjects"—as free
beings; and such a look does not threaten the bourgeoisie
and does not produce the desire for unity with other
bourgeoisie members. It is only when the proletarian class
becomes powerful and begins to threaten the power of
the bourgeois class that the bourgeoisie also attains a class
consciousness under the "look" of the now vital and threat-
ening proletariat.

Thus the oppression that a member of the proletariat
suffers is a double one: he suffers the oppression of economic exploitation, and he suffers the humiliating oppression of being looked upon as an object—a thing. And it is
the latter oppression, according to Sartre, more than the
former that gives rise to the proletariat's class consciousness and class unity.

Sartre does not stop at this somewhat negative definition
of class and class consciousness; he envisions a more positive class consciousness in the worker's refusal to be made
into an object, and in his pursuance of the subjective
goals of his being. (By nature every man is a subject,
never an object; when he accepts a definition of himself
as an object he is deceiving himself as to his true nature.
The terminology here and throughout this section is tricky

and misleading unless one keeps in mind the existential definition of "subject" as the *pour-soi*—consciousness, and of "object" as the *en-soi*—the material world.) By pursuing the subjective goals of his being the worker surmounts the oppression and actively aims at the realization of a society which will guarantee him his subjectivity, his freedom as a man.

Class unity, then, is apparently achieved by a twofold and opposed movement: the unity brought about by the gaze of the privileged, and the unity brought about by the rejection of that disparaging gaze and a desire to become free of it. It is the last part of this process—the becoming free of the gaze—and the more important part as far as a philosophy of revolution is concerned, that is the more doubtful and less tenable one; although the first part—the class unity brought about by the gaze—does not escape criticism either. Granted that the look of a superior, or rather privileged person may turn another person into an object; but the latter still has equal freedom, according to Existentialist tenets, to look down at the former with all his privileges and so to make an object out of him as well. The argument that the privileged and the leaders are not looked upon as objects by their inferiors is a specious one, given the philosophy's basic premise that all men are equally free in all things. Since when did a hierarchy of "looks" arise? If there is such a hierarchy then, in contradiction to Existentialism, by nature some men are more free than others. The alternative possibility is that classes and class consciousness are a result of a struggle of looks: which group can stare down the other with greater indignation. It must be mentioned here that the "look" is not merely a gaze but a syndrome including in itself various norms and values, in this case class norms and values. Thus when a bourgeois "looks" at members of the proletariat he sees them as depraved, worthless, etc.; and when a proletarian "looks" at members of the bourgeoisie he

sees them as privileged and himself as not recognized, as
discriminated against, etc. Yet nevertheless, "looks," and
the responses to them, are an individual and a subjective
phenomenon, and as such they cannot produce concrete
classes. Individual members of the bourgeoisie look at individual members of the proletariat; a number of the proletarian members become aware of the look and realize
their poverty and lack of privileges. Why should this
cause them to unite? Some of them may even think it
right and good that the bourgeoisie has greater privileges;
others may not feel their lack of privileges as a deprivation; and still others may deem the bourgeois a slave to
his wealth and privileges and so make him into an object
by their look. Who is the oppressed now, and where is
the proletarian solidarity produced by the bourgeois gaze?

And what about the second aspect that aids class unity,
the rejection of the look as an object-making thing and the
desire to change the situation so that one becomes a subject and free? Here two separate motions are needed: the
rejection of the look, and the desire to become a free subject through a change of the material situation. How, then,
is class unity achieved? Some workers may reject the look
and, in turn, see the bourgeois as an object; others may
accept it and live in bad faith and self-deception; and
only a few may both reject it and attempt to change the
situation.

Also, throughout this discussion of workers' solidarity it
is necessary to remember the existential ontology which
holds that the most fundamental relationship among men
is always individual conflict where everyone is an object
for everyone else, never a subject.

The conceptions of the origin of classes and of class-
consciousness outlined and criticized above are given in
Being and Nothingness, and they differ to some extent
from the simpler formulation given in "Materialism and
Revolution." In this essay, published three years after *Being and Nothingness*, Sartre argues that the unity of the

working class arises because the individual worker realizes that, as a worker, he can never become integrated with the privileged classes, and therefore is compelled to act for the liberation of his entire class. Through this realization on the part of each individual worker proletarian solidarity is achieved. This somewhat less mystical view than the one described in *Being and Nothingness* does not, however, invalidate the argument that classes, class-consciousness, and class unity are the result of the "look" of disdain by the bourgeoisie prompted by the workers' backward economic condition. And Sartre apparently maintains both views.

The criticisms of the "look" theory in the preceding paragraphs might be made by any Marxist, who would most certainly add that Sartre's understanding of class, class consciousness, and the revolutionary is contrary to the historical, economic, and sociological facts discovered by Marx in his studies of the origin of classes, class consciousness, class struggles, and the causes of revolutions. By Sartre's definition of the revolutionary and of the revolutionary situation, it is not necessarily true that only the worker is in a position to become a revolutionary, since not only economic exploitation, but also social status, race, nationality, and membership in an organization are possible sources of the humiliating type of oppression which makes man an object in the Sartrean sense. Also, a revolution by one of these oppressed groups would not mean that a classless society would come into being, for the oppressed class—be it Negroes, colonists, or some other group—may simply wish to turn the tables and rule over its former masters; and this would fulfill Sartre's criterion that a revolution must bring about a change in institutions and property rights. The Marxist would likewise question whether Sartre's logically untenable conclusion that the proletariat is the *only* revolutionary force, is not an *a posteriori* argument and a borrowing from Marxism.

Nor could Marxists ever consent to the Existentialist definitions of the revolutionary and the revolution, of class and class consciousness as being subjective and, in the last analysis, individual and not group phenomena, only indirectly connected with the economic situation. The "look" of the bourgeoisie may indeed be disturbing to the proletariat, but this minor detail of human relations is not what unites it and drives it to revolution: only economic conditions can create such uniting and revolutionary forces; and it is the economic situation that is responsible for the "look" as well. Besides, the "look" of the bourgeoisie is often charitable and humanistic, even though the charity and the humanism are misplaced if there is no understanding that it is the economic situation that requires humanistic change.

Finally, Marxists would point to the contradiction in the Existentialist theory, which, on the one hand, claims interpersonal conflict among all men as one of its ontological principles, and then attempts to speak of class unity and class solidarity. Given the ontology, the conflict must be more violent among persons who know each other and work with each other than among persons who are strangers to each other. The personal conflict among the members of the same organization (for example, a union, in the case of workers) should be more violent than the conflict among the opposed classes. What could perhaps control this intragroup conflict—strong pressure from another group—is also invalidated, for the factors which unite the members into a class are primarily individual and subjective: the individual's realization and choice to act for the benefit of the entire class, or the individual's rejection of the "look" of the superior class and desire to unite with others to change the social and economic conditions which gave rise to that "look."

The Marxists, therefore, can see very little validity and consistency in Sartre's ideas on the whole problem of classes, class-consciousness, and the revolutionary and his situation. And this conclusion on their part is warranted by an examination of the theories involved.

The Revolutionary Philosophy

After his exposition of the revolutionary and his situation, Sartre develops further the topic of revolution and materialism and their relation to each other. He has defined the revolutionary—as an oppressed person who is indispensable to a society exactly in his oppressed function and who acts to change the society in order to do away with his oppression—and he now wishes to provide this revolutionary with a philosophy. He approaches the problem through an analysis of the philosophical needs of the revolutionary. And at the same time he indicates how materialism is not able to supply those theoretical needs.

He finds, therefore, that a true revolutionary demands a philosophy which will do the following:

1. Explain history, society, man, and values as transient, not guided by any Providence, and capable of being changed for the better.

2. Remove any special divine privileges from all men and so produce natural equality for all, which is but another definition of humanism.

3. Make action the means of both understanding and changing the world; and explain reality as a material fact and not some abstract idealistic concept.

4. Give man freedom and ability to make his own laws, values, ends; to transcend the present situation and to carve his own pathway into a future that is not predetermined.

From these prescriptions, says Sartre, it is evident why revolutionaries have often favored a materialistic philosophy. From the earliest times, those who wished to bring about man's liberation in any aspect of life or thought have usually relied upon materialism for support, e.g.,

Epicurus, Lucretius, and many others. Sartre acknowledges this debt to materialism, but still maintains that upon closer examination materialism is a liability rather than an asset for a philosophy of revolution. To substantiate his thesis he proceeds to a more detailed description of a revolutionary's needs, and follows this with an examination of materialism's influence upon those needs.

Beginning with the first point, he finds, therefore, that the revolutionary goes beyond his present situation to a new situation; the revolutionary sees history as a process, a progressive movement, and himself as the agent of history capable of bringing about this progress. He thinks hard; he acts; he loathes the idealistic tendency to see changes in the world as changes in ideas: "death, unemployment, strike-suppression, poverty and hunger are not ideas. They are everyday realities that are experienced in horror."[6]

Second, being a worker, in order to accomplish any historical transition he must remove all Providential, divine interference with or guidance of history and society; similarly, he must reject any claims of the ruling class to divine rights and privileges. History, man, and values must all be made natural and relative, produced either by nature or by man. He declares that he, too, is a man like all other men, not different in any basic principle, who also has the equal right and ability to do what all other men do. Thus, "his humanism is not based on human dignity, but, on the contrary, denies man any particular dignity."[7] He reduces all men to the human species.

Third, he must refuse to recognize the primacy of knowledge as a *contemplation* of the universe, for such a vision produces a conservative, static view of the world and society; instead he must develop a theory of knowledge which unites thought and action and shows "that action is the unmasking [understanding] of reality, and, *at the same time*, a modification of that reality."[8]

And fourth, the revolutionary must be unencumbered

by any determinism, either divine or philosophical, so that
he can be free to leave his present situation and create
his own laws in the development of a more favorable situation in the future.

In all these respects, in his conception of history, of society, of man, of values, of knowledge, of action, and of
freedom, materialism seems to answer the revolutionary's
needs. But in reality it gives him more than he asked for,
claims Sartre. The revolutionary pulls all down to nature,
but the materialist's attitude toward nature is ambiva-
lent. On the one hand, he, too, drags all things to the
natural level, both slaves and masters, but then he pro-
claims that he wants to set up a rational human organization to replace what nature had produced blindly:

> The Marxist expression for designating the society
> of the future is *antiphysis*. This means that Marxists
> want to set up a human order whose laws will con-
> stitute the negation of natural laws. And we are
> probably to understand by this that this order will be
> produced only by obeying the prescriptions of Na-
> ture. But the fact is that this order must *be conceived*
> within a Nature that denies it; the fact is that in the
> anti-Natural society the conception of law will pre-
> cede the establishment of law, whereas, at present,
> law, according to materialism, conditions our concep-
> tion of it.[9]

Again, materialism aids the revolutionary by explaining
the "upper by the lower," and in this fashion it makes him
the support of the entire society: it is he, as the worker,
who is characterized by the economic, the technological,
and the biological. It also provides a myth, Sartre says, of
the more complex coming from the simple, and so it lib-
erates him from his fears because it gives simple and
knowable causes for all phenomena. All these beliefs, then,
help to justify the revolutionary attitude. But once more
materialism betrays the revolutionary, for the explanation

of the "upper by the lower" turns both the master and the slave into things, because direct material causation transforms all men into behavior patterns. (Thus, at the same time, materialism plays into the master's hands, for that is exactly how the master views the worker.) The materialistic explanation forgets that the revolutionary is not interested in becoming a thing or an object but in mastering things and objects.

Materialism, with its strong implications of determinism, ends all useful activity toward progress in history, another fact that is contrary to revolutionary requirements. It eliminates resistance to reality because natural laws are determined in advance, and all that remains is to decipher history, not to make it. This is in opposition to revolutionary realism, which sees every progressive step as a difficult struggle with the outcome not certain. A revolutionary does not want his path cleared by history; he wants to clear it himself.

In action, materialism also seems to answer his demands, for it places matter over the idea: it is realistic. But besides placing matter over ideas, the revolutionary needs examples of resistance being overcome, and nature provides no proofs that resistance can be overcome: when force is applied it reacts according to the laws of mechanics. What is more, "in order to account for reality as a resistance to be overcome by work, this resistance must be experienced by a subjectivity that seeks to subdue it. Nature conceived as pure objectivity is the opposite of the idea. But precisely because of this, it becomes transformed into idea; it is the pure idea of objectivity. The *real* vanishes."[10] Therefore in the end it is not only idealism but also materialism that causes the real to disappear: "the one because it eliminates the object, the other because it eliminates subjectivity."[11] A revolutionary requires both the objective existence of the world and his own subjectivity, which will give him the ability to act on and against that world. Once more, materialism by seeing only objectivity gives the revolutionary more than he bargained for.

Materialism likewise forbids the making of value judgments concerning the activities of the adversaries of the revolutionary: a bourgeois and his actions are only the products of materially imposed necessity. A revolutionary cannot accept such a restriction. Also, materialism as an interpretation of history and of the world becomes useless in the classless society where neither an upper nor a lower grouping exists; it can never bring about a humanist, which means subjective, organization of society; it can only produce a rational organization, which is a fetter on human (subjective) freedom and therefore incompatible with humanism. And lastly, materialism falls short of a revolutionary theory of knowledge because it renders all thought a product of social and material conditions, and "the idea of a conditioned thinking is self-destructive."[12]

The revolutionary has another great need, which materialism is also incapable of giving him—freedom, the possibility of transcending the present. For it is only when the oppressed person by a movement of transcendence challenges the rights and the ideology of the oppressors that he becomes a revolutionary. And the possibility of transcendence cannot be found in a person's natural and material existence, for he must put these in the past and judge his existence from the point of view of the future. This possibility of *"rising above* a situation in order to get a perspective on it . . . is precisely that which we call freedom."[13] And freedom, which is also man's possession of his own future destiny, is the major goal of the revolutionary. In order to obtain freedom, to be free, man must be able to replace the given laws—both natural and social—by the ends he desires: he must be able to invent his own laws.

Materialism's inability to provide freedom for the revolutionary is its greatest lack. Materialism, with its cause and effect, its laws of behaviorism, can never explain the

possibility of *rising above* a situation—a material situation
at that—and looking back upon it in its totality with a desire to re-create it. Dialectical materialism attempts to explain such a thrust toward the future, but it ascribes freedom to things, not to man, and that is absurd. Neither
materialism nor dialectical materialism is capable of
producing a revolutionary class-consciousness. Marxists
know this; that is why they rely upon a group of militants
to awaken this consciousness in the masses. Materialism,
like Samson, buries both the oppressor and the revolutionary in the inert denseness of matter, where no freedom can exist. "For facts can only generate facts, and
not the representation of facts; the present generates another present, not the future."[14] And the revolutionary,
in order to be successful, must have the contingent quality
of the fact, but at the same time in practice be able to
transcend the fact, i.e., the given situation of the present.

In the face of all the actualities listed, Sartre concludes
that a revolutionary philosophy demands much more than
materialism can ever provide. However, idealism is not
the answer either, for it is mainly a conservative point of
view toward the world and too abstract to be useful; for
example, when it speaks of freedom it sees it as an internal condition and not an external fact. Thus idealism deceives the revolutionary because "it binds him with rights
and values that are already given; it conceals from him
his power to blaze his own path. But materialism, by
robbing him of his freedom, also deceives him. Revolutionary philosophy should be a philosophy of transcendence."[15]

Again, both idealism and materialism are "monistic"
philosophies, unable to account for either a theory of violence, which a revolutionary philosophy must do, or the
plurality of conflicting freedoms. Idealism sanctions violence only in support of the present order, which it sees
as based upon monolithic, absolutistic values; materialism,
by reducing men and oppression to the laws of mechanics,

of forces acting upon forces, cannot account for a conflict of opposites, which a theory of violence also demands. Materialism is monistic, Sartre claims, because there is no conflict of opposites in matter: hot and cold are not opposites; they simply reflect different degrees of temperature, etc. Marxism projects the idea of a conflict of opposites from human relations upon material relations.

Having therefore dismissed both materialism and idealism as unsuited for a philosophy of revolution, Sartre provides a short recipe for the basic elements of such a philosophy. In reading the statement it is impossible to mistake which philosophy it is that he finds adequate for a revolutionary purpose:

> A revolutionary philosophy ought to account for the plurality of freedoms and show how each one can be an object for the other while being, at the same time, a freedom for itself. Only this double character of freedom and objectivity can explain the complex notions of oppression, conflict, failure and violence. For one never oppresses anything but a freedom, but one cannot oppress it if it lends itself in some way to this oppression, if, that is, it presents the appearance of a thing to the Other. The revolutionary movement and its plan—which is to make society pass through the violence of one state in which liberties are alienated to another state based on their mutual recognition—is to be understood in these terms.[16]

We recognize here a description of the Existentialist theory of the free individual as a subject for himself and an object for all others, with the resulting conflict of wills. It would appear, then, that Existentialism is the only philosophy fully competent to provide a theory of revolution. Sartre does not state this conclusion openly, but the implications are impossible to mistake. And this is not the first time that he implies the role of the Third Party for

Existentialism—as a philosophy that transcends, or even achieves the synthesis of, idealism and materialism.

Sartre had already assigned himself the task of such a transcendence of the dualism of idealism and materialism in *Being and Nothingness,* where he made an attempt to surmount most of the traditional dualisms: interior-exterior, appearance-essence, and *en-soi-pour-soi* or the world and man.[17] And at the beginning of "Materialism and Revolution" he criticizes those who reject "with the contemptuous name of 'Third Party' the synthesis which embraces them [idealism and materialism]."[18] Again, near the end of the first part of this essay, he calls materialism a useful myth for a politician; but he argues that if the politician is interested in a long-range affair he needs not a myth but the *Truth.* And he assigns the task of piecing together the truths contained in materialism to the philosopher, so that the true philosophy will suit the needs of the revolution as well as the myth does. Again it is not difficult to find the philosopher Sartre is speaking of. And in reply to those who hold that a union of the two diametrically opposed philosophies is impossible, he calls upon Marx for support, claiming that "in 1844 he wrote that the antinomy between idealism and materialism would have to be transcended."[19]

Having thus established his case for the need and the possibility of a philosophical third party, he launches into a laudatory oration on the new revolutionary philosophy—still not calling it Existentialism—which "transcending both idealist thinking which is bourgeois and the myth of materialism which suited the oppressed masses for a while, claims to be the philosophy of *man* in the general sense."[20] It is a philosophy that eliminates all classes and does not struggle for the preservation of one class only: it is for the unity of all men. It is a philosophy, therefore, that can be understood by all, even the bourgeois, who through it can recognize that by the oppression of other freedoms he is a victim of his own oppression, that his freedom can be asserted only by the recognition bestowed on it by other freedoms. It is a philosophy of humanism *par excellence;* and it is the philosophy of truth: "Not the abstract Truth of idealism [or the ambiguous truth of Marxism, which at one time is a class truth and at another time an absolute truth], but concrete truth, willed, created, maintained, and conquered through social struggle by men who work at the liberation of man."[21]

Today, Marxism, Sartre writes in concluding his examination of materialism and revolution, is passing through a crisis: Marxists are caught in a dilemma because of the obsolescence of the materialist myth and the fear of creating a division in their ranks by the adoption of a new ideology. They remain with materialism, thinking that it does not matter since their struggle is predominantly a political one. They may be correct for the present, "but," says Sartre, "what kind of men are they forming? You cannot, with impunity, form generations of men by imbuing them with successful, but false, ideas. What will happen if materialism stifles the revolutionary design to death one day?"[22]

Before commencing a detailed critique of Sartre's arguments against materialism as a pernicious theory for a revolutionary philosophy, Marxists would first of all point out that Sartre's entire orientation in the essay on revolution and materialism, contrary to his claims near the end of that essay, is not toward an examination of what is factual and true, but of what is useful.

Sartre, according to his own admission in the essay, criticizes materialism mainly because it fails to satisfy the needs of a revolutionary; whether it is a true explanation of the world interests him only indirectly. In this way, he himself indulges in the opportunism of which he accuses Marxism when he speaks of its pragmatic adoption of the "materialist myth." Yet all that he has done is created a myth of his own: the myth of a revolutionary and his revolution. And then he has proceeded to supply the myth with both its needs and the answers to those needs. Thus, besides being opportunistic, the entire argument takes place on an abstract level, never touching the real historical conditions of the past or the practical needs of the present: there is no reference to concrete political, economic, social, or historical facts of how a real revolutionary situation develops, what causes it, and what are the possible actions in such a situation.

It is an easy task first to decide abstractly what the particular needs are in an abstract formulation of a theory of revolution and then to supply equally abstract answers to those needs. And in this entire procedure, Sartre acts more like a politician interested in discrediting his opposition—materialism and Marxism—than like a philosopher interested mainly in discovering what is true. His criterion for a revolutionary philosophy is not truth, but success and victory in the revolutionary struggle. Now there may be nothing wrong with that, but it scarcely justifies Sartre for accusing Marxism of adopting the materialist myth for the sake of revolutionary success.

After this general preface, Marxists would then examine Sartre's arguments in greater detail.

First, Sartre, for the sake of his arguments, constantly pushes the materialistic theory to an absurd and untenable position: he interprets it much too narrowly. He speaks, for example, of nature, of natural law, of causation, as mechanical entities; he makes all things into objects to which only the quantitative laws of mechanics apply. When it comes to his own arguments concerning the subjective freedom of the individual and the objective, determined conditions in which that individual must act, Sartre sees no opposition "between these two necessities of action, namely that the agent be free and that the world in which he acts be determined."[23] Yet he refuses to grant to Marxism, which does not demand absolute individual freedom but only a partial one, even a modified version of his statement: that there is no contradiction in a determined world and the ability to act, to a certain extent, freely upon that world.

Regardless of what Sartre says, there is no contradiction either in the materialistic belief that a rational human order can be substituted for the blind order produced by nature, that the laws of nature can be regulated. Sartre would not deny that science has been able to regulate the laws of nature for its purposes, or that human societies often operate according to laws and causes of which men are not conscious, but that when they do attain to consciousness of them they may influence and change them. This, he certainly knows, has been the position of Marxism from its inception. Natural and social causation is not a fetter on man's ability to act in the world; on the contrary, it is encouraging: writes a philosopher, "it gives me something to do. . . . It invites the play of reason. Where there are causes, mind can operate; preventions can be worked out."[24]

How do such interpretations of the world harm a theory of revolution? Do they not instead make it real and possible? It would be interesting to discover how Existentialism wishes to solve this problem with its conception of the world as chaotic, lawless, and causeless. Certainly under these conditions no rational organization of society is possible, and neither can revolutionary action have any concrete effect upon a world and a society that never pause long enough in their chaotic whirling for an action to produce the desired result. Existentialism, then, flagrantly contradicts itself. How can Sartre declare at one time that he is a materialist, and imply that the material world acts according to determined laws, and at another time write that the material world is an amorphous, nausea-producing mass? The distinction between these two is not unimportant; which view of the universe one holds makes a great deal of difference for a social theory.

Sartre further accuses materialism of reducing all men to objects, to mechanical robots. Again he ignores the fact that Marxism recognizes man's subjectivity; it is only "vulgar" Marxists who interpret the natural and economic laws and causes as mechanical actions upon human consciousness. And it is because of the recognized subjectivity of men that Marxism permits ethical criticism. If men were totally irresponsible for their actions, Sartre would be correct in declaring that no value judgments of such actions are possible. But it is Marx who wrote that men make their own history. This is also the reason why the consciousness of men must be awakened, why they must be directed to act, for nothing happens of itself; history and progress are the results only of the concrete actions of men.

Instead of accusing Marxism of turning men into objects because of its theory of materialism, Sartre might reflect on his own Existentialist ontology, which really does turn all men into objects (with conflict as the basis of their relationship). The fact that each man is a subject for himself does not obviate the "objective" character of all human and social relations, in which men are *things* for each other.

The greatest fault Sartre finds in materialism is that it annihilates the revolutionary's cause by denying him freedom, or the power of transcending his present situation. It would be repetitious to review the Marxist conception of freedom not as a dream of escaping natural laws and causes but as being conditioned by the given environment, yet at the same time allowing for the alteration of many laws once one is in possession of the principles guiding their operations. It is more profitable to state that transcendence can come only from what exists in the present, that a vacuum can produce nothing, that therefore any future must be shaped in and by the present, for what more is it than an extension and a prolongation of the present? (This does not, of course, exclude qualitative changes, but that is a matter of little relevance to the present discussion.) Marx has provided students of society with objective criteria for a scientific judgment concerning future social development. What Existentialism has to offer for the future would remain a mystery if it were not a simple matter to deduce a state of anarchy from its philosophical views.

Lastly, Sartre's equating of idealism and materialism as both being absolutistic, idealistic, and monistic, and his proposal of Existentialism as a superior synthesis of the two, a synthesis with revolutionary activism and universal truth at its command, are somewhat pretentious arguments, not deserving of too serious attention. His turning of materialism into idealism is accomplished by an apparently sophistic argument: if nature is conceived as purely objective, then it is the opposite of an idea, and therefore it is transformed into a pure idea of objectivity. This argument is certainly quite poor for a serious philosopher, who knows well what materialism's claims are. The question that Sartre should answer is whether nature is an objective fact or a subjective idea. That is the manner in which Marxism states the problem, and, according to the answer given, divides the materialists from the idealists. Marxism does not refuse to recognize that man perceives nature subjectively and often impresses his desires and longings upon it and even attempts to change it so that it accords with those desires and longings. But the point remains that the world, nature, is an objective fact; it is the truth of this proposition that may be challenged, and its truth is not obliterated by an argument that purports to turn facts into ideas.

What is Existentialism's answer to the above question? Is it a materialistic philosophy or an idealistic one? Existentialism claims to achieve a synthesis of the two, but all it actually achieves is the confusion of the entire matter: at one time the world is an objective fact with given

laws, at another it is that which the mind and the will of
the subjective individual make of it. But which is it? It
cannot be both at one and the same time. Since Existentialists refuse to answer the question unequivocally, since
they wish to play a game of hide-and-seek with the objective world, Marxists answer for them. Existentialism
with its emphasis upon the subjective, extra-historical,
absolutely free individual, denies the facts of the objective world, of objective historical and social conditions,
and therefore qualifies as an idealistic philosophy.

Existentialism propounds the claim that only it can account for the conflicts of society and so justify revolutionary thought and action. Materialism, it discloses, is
monistic, for nature has no opposites, only variations in
degree—as if the proton $(+)$ and the electron $(-)$, or the
positive and negative poles of a magnet were not in opposition—and must borrow the idea of opposed forces in
conflict from society. And this Existentialist claim to an
improved theory of social conflict is given with the
knowledge of Marxism, whose founder is known particularly for the theory that history is but a series of conflicts
among opposed classes. It is true that Existentialist philosophy can account for conflict in society, a ceaseless
conflict among all members, an endless war of all against
all. But the more important question is whether Existentialism can account for harmony and solidarity in a class,
and later in the classless society. Marxism with its materialism is able to account for these things more easily than
Existentialism with its idealistic theory of man's damna-
tion to eternal conflict with all other men.

Before closing this chapter on the revolution, several
comments are in order.

In his attack on materialism as unsuited to revolutionary purposes, Sartre does not indicate clearly whether
he is speaking of independent materialism, dialectical
materialism, the Marxist use of materialism, or all three

combined. He indiscriminately flies from materialism, to dialectics, to Marxism, whichever he finds more appropriate for his argument at the moment. Because of this, his arguments are often incoherent and follow no specific plan. He argues in the style of a rhetorician rather than that of a philosopher: instead of seeking the truth he seems to be more interested in creating a hurried, emotional impression and so gaining victory in the argument. In this, he does injustice to himself, to the argument against Marxism, and to his claim of disclosing a truth more valid than the Marxist one. Needless to say, Marxism cannot be disproved by a distortion of its tenets but only through a sincere examination of its doctrines as they are really presented.

On the other hand, Sartre adopts, in a modified manner, several Marxist ideas, particularly the definition of the revolutionary and the revolutionary situation as being, in the last analysis, products of economic oppression. He therefore opens himself to the usual criticisms of Marxism: its refusal to admit that the oppression of the working class in industrialized countries is being eliminated; that a large middle class is thriving and not becoming a part of any "deprived" proletariat; that mobility among classes exists and is possible; that ownership is becoming widely dispersed; that government controls aid the worker, etc. These arguments would not, however, be conclusive against Sartre, because while adopting certain Marxist concepts he also holds a more ethereal definition of the revolutionary, his class consciousness, and his revolution; and the existential definition would be able to account for all these criticisms. The "look" is even more powerful than the economic environment in determining oppression: a worker does not have to suffer economic deprivation in order to be oppressed; his *status* as a worker is sufficient to cause oppression. But here Sartre has left Marxist definitions for definitions even less tenable, as the criticism given in the earlier part of this chapter demonstrated.

For the sake of his argument, Sartre has also too lightly dismissed idealism as a revolutionary force; many revolutions described in history were motivated not by materialistic doctrines but by idealistic and, especially, religious theories: one of the earliest rebellions noted in history, that of Moses against the Egyptian Pharaoh, was inspired by religious ideals, as was the revolt of the Maccabees against the Romans, and later the rebellion of Jan Huss, and that of the Puritans in England.

As far as the synthesis of idealism and materialism is concerned, Sartre does not manage to bridge the gap, despite his claims to the contrary. In other writings he admits that the union is an impossible one. In his philosophy the *pour-soi* represents the subjective and idealistic element and the *en-soi*, the objective and materialistic element, and there is a yearning in man to achieve a union of the two. Such a union is "a consciousness which would be foundation of its own being-*en-soi* by the pure consciousness that it would take of itself,"[25] which could only be what is understood by God.

Because the yearning of man for such a union—for the *pour-soi* to lose itself in order to find its own being in the *en-soi*—is impossible, since man is not God, "the *pour-soi* loses itself in vain: 'man is a useless passion.'"[26] The synthesis of idealism with materialism, in the being who is most able to achieve such a union, is an impossibility. And if it cannot be attained in existence, neither can it be accomplished validly in thought, for then by definition it would still be idealism.

Existentialism's claim to third party status is thus invalidated, as is its claim to universal truth, since in Existentialism truth is even more subjective than in Marxism: it is purely individual, whereas in Marxism it is at least a class truth.

One wonders exactly what Sartre is attempting to say

in the matter of truth and revolution. He mentions, for
example, the Marxist use of the Catholic argument of
asking how the practical success of the doctrine can be
explained if it is theoretically erroneous. And he adds,
"this argument, which is scholastic, and which offers an
a posteriori proof in terms of success, *is far from insignificant*"[27] (italics added). In a later paragraph he writes:
"Materialism is indisputably the *only myth* that suits revolutionary requirements"[28] (italics in the original). Why
then does he attack it and attempt to find a substitute
for it? His avowed reason seems to be a search after truth,
not a truth for the moment, but a truth valid in the long
run also. Yet from the method of his argumentation such
a conclusion would be difficult to reach. On the contrary,
it seems that he dislikes the materialistic myth and
wants to replace it with a myth that conforms better to
Existentialism. But why do that if he admits that the materialist myth is the only efficacious one at the present
time? Especially when he says that he knows that man
has no salvation other than in the liberation of the working class, and that he knows that the intellectuals' interest lies with the proletariat?[29] What is his purpose in such
a substitution? According to his own standards he would
be betraying all mankind by providing an abstract, un-
tried, and therefore weaker weapon for the working class.
To be consistent he must do the same thing he accuses
the Marxists of doing: he must sacrifice the abstract truth
in the present for a better truth in the future. Of what
use is his long-run *Truth* when it may never see the light
of the future if the present struggle is lost? Logically,
instead of doing disservice to mankind by attacking materialism, he should rather defend it and help to sharpen
its arguments so that it may become even a stronger
weapon, a more powerful myth.

Finally, had Sartre been less interested in a political
argument and more in a serious philosophical discussion,
he could have, for example, legitimately raised the issue

that Marxism is ambiguous in its conception of history and the individual's role in it, either as actor or as revolutionary. It cannot decide whether history is determined or whether it is truly made by man. From here he could have argued that such ambiguity is harmful for revolutionary activity, for it may easily lead to quietism and passivity, permitting time to do its work, or that, because of the ambiguity, it must first convince men that they should act in order to realize their hopes. The question of action, both Marxist and Existentialist, will be developed further in the sixth chapter.

chapter five

HISTORICAL, SOCIOLOGICAL, AND PSYCHOLOGICAL CRITIQUES

Having established the fundamental tenets of Marxism and Existentialism and reviewed some of their more specific doctrines and disagreements, we may turn to more general critiques attacking each philosophy, not in its particulars but in its entirety and from various vantage points—historical, sociological, psychological. Because of the very broad nature of these critiques, a possible analysis of them would necessarily also indulge in generalities and therefore fail to meet scholarly standards. Thus, for example, when Sartre claims that Marxism is characterized by a religious character and that it justifies itself only in the realm of faith, or when B. Dunham seriously argues that Existentialism is a psychological illness, the arguments are difficult to refute or even analyze on scholarly grounds, particularly since these statements are meant to apply to the entire philosophy and not merely to specific parts of it. The arguments are made in the nature of general critical statements and observations rather than in the nature of philosophical arguments and must be understood and treated as such.

The critiques in this chapter are given, then, for the sake of completeness and for their intrinsic interest. Wherever possible, remarks will be made concerning their broad validity and any other points of value to which they may give rise. In this respect, it is interesting to note, that on both sides the criticisms fall into equivalent cate-

gories: each finds in the other remains of religious principles, a reflection of objective social conditions with
some type of remedy for these conditions, and a denial of
scientific method and truth.

Beginning with Existentialist opinion, we find Sartre
continuing the arguments already intimated in the preceding chapter. He thinks that Marxists who characterize
their philosophy as a "human *attitude*" are correct, and
he speaks of having witnessed "conversions" to materialism and Marxism. With approval he quotes Marxism
as declaring that new ideas and social theories arise as a
response to new social tasks and needs; he quotes Stalin
as claiming that Marxism-Leninism is strong because it
answers the practical needs of the people; and Sartre
therefore concludes that Marxism with its materialism is
a doctrine of utility and that its truth is pragmatic and
relative. But then Marxism is an *opinion,* whose truth is
measured in its power of action, yet it is a strange opinion
—one that also claims to be certitude, and it therefore:

> carries within it its own destuction, for it is obliged,
> in the very name of its principles, to regard itself as
> an objective fact, as a reflection of being, as an ob-
> ject of science, and, at the same time, it destroys the
> science which should analyze and establish it—at
> least as an opinion. The circle is obvious, and the
> whole system remains suspended in air, perpetually
> floating between being and nothingness.[1]

The way out of the circle for the Marxist is through
faith. "He believes in Marx, Lenin and Stalin, he admits
of the principle of authority, and, finally, he retains the
blind and tranquil faith in the certitude of Marxism."[2]
If one attempts to analyze his doctrines in detail, he will
retort that he has no time to waste on trifles, for the situation is urgent and he must act: first things first. And so
the opinion turns into indisputable fact. His program is
not unlike Pascal's: "Fall to thy knees and thou shalt

believe."³ It is little wonder that as a believer he is suspicious of the scientist, who rejects the principle of authority, who challenges all beliefs and constantly demands empirical or rational proof. Yet the mistrust remains guarded, for, practically, he also needs the scientist with all these dubious virtues.

Albert Camus in *The Rebel* takes up this religious aspect of Marxism and develops it further. He calls Marxism a Messianism and a prophecy. He views present-day Marxism as having discarded the founder's critical method and turned more and more to his prophecies; instead of adapting the theory to the facts Marxists now attempt to adapt the facts to the prophecy:

> It can be said of Marx that the greater part of his predictions came into conflict with facts as soon as his prophecies began to become an object of increasing faith. The reason is simple: the predictions were short-term and could be controlled. . . . When the predictions failed to come true, the prophecies remained the only hope; with the result that they alone rule over our history.⁴

After this preliminary statement, Camus traces Marxism to its origins in Christian and bourgeois world-views and ideals. He discovers a close correlation between the Marxist and the Christian view of nature and history, with Marxism adopting the Christian attitudes. Both Marxism and Christianity consider the history of man unique and aiming toward a given end; both think of nature as only the setting for the historical drama, and as a thing that must be subdued, conquered, and enslaved —certainly not passively obeyed. In this they diverge greatly from the Greek attitude, which saw history as a cycle and nature as beneficial, beautiful, and a source of learning. Yet so long as a belief existed in the divinity of Christ, a mediation between man and nature was possible. When Christ became only a symbol of the man-god, mediation ceased and the Judaic world reappeared. It is this world that Marxism has inherited. And in the now-Godless world ". . . the implacable god of war rules again; all beauty is insulated as the source of idle pleasures, nature itself is enslaved. Marx, from this point of view, is the Jeremiah of the god of history and the Saint Augustine of the revolution."[5] That explains, argues Camus, why a close relation exists between the Catholic reactionary philosopher DeMaistre and Marx. Both put an end to the divisions between essence and existence, freedom and necessity. Both speak to man in an ambiguous manner—telling him that he must act as if he could do all things and at the same time resign himself as if he could do nothing. DeMaistre justifies the established order; Marx justifies the order to come: "The most eloquent eulogy of capitalism was made by its greatest enemy. Marx is only anti-capitalist in so far as capitalism is out of date."[6] In politics both rely upon the same methods—political realism, discipline, force. Both are religious: one believes in God; the other deifies man, since socialism makes man the supreme being for man. Even though at the beginning they may be widely separated, in reality they merely use different symbols, and so in the end are united by the same conclusions.

The Marxist retort to these arguments is that Existentialists know well the teachings of Marx on religion, faith, and Christianity, and that as far as conversions are concerned, it is an area in which Existentialism specializes. Existentialism preaches a change of consciousness, a change in life from the unauthentic existence to the authentic existence. And Marxists in turn, proceed to trace Existentialism to its origin in religion. They find that the first real exponent of Existentialism, Soren Kierkegaard, was a minister.[7] Thus it is easy to conclude that the differentiation between man's true and non-true being is of Christian origin, as is the view of death as a means of attaining true being and true ethical conduct in life. Marxists reverse Camus' argument and disclose that it is Existentialism and Christianity that differ radically from the Greeks in their conceptions of nature, history, the individual personality, the individual's relation to the rest of society, and even in the attitude toward death. In contrast to the optimistic world-view of the Greeks, in which the individual was a part of the entire cosmos, in which death was of minor importance, Christianity pessimistically saw the world as a place of suffering, of individual alienation from nature, history, society, other men, and conceived of death as the focal point of man's existence. Again, mediation was achieved in the belief in a God and an eternal life; but when modern society came to doubt these beliefs only the somber principles remained. And it is these that Existentialism has inherited—the Judaic world without the Christian God:

> the existentialists, both of the atheistic and the religious variety, represent in fact the same position and reiterate the cruelty and perversity of the old Jehovah. They also construe the Individual as allegedly sovereign, but only to make him lonely, to isolate him from society, to reduce to despair and forlornness those miserable, ridiculous little worms wriggling helplessly under foot of malicious Fate with fool's crowns of sovereignty on their heads.[8]

It is not Marxism but Existentialism, then, that makes a god out of the individual, but because Christ, the man-god, who could have led all men to godhood has been rejected, the Existentialist man-god is a chained and tortured god. And lastly, it is Existentialism that serves the reactionary element, either by default, as in the case of Sartre's Existentialism which contains no social theory at all, or by choice, as in the case of the frankly religious Existentialists and Heidegger.

Returning for the moment to further Existentialist critiques, this time aimed at Marxism's origin, we find Camus arguing that Marxism contains a scientific Messianism which it borrowed from bourgeois myths. "Progress, the future of science, the cult of technology and of production, are bourgeois myths, which in the nineteenth century became dogma."[9] All these were the hopes of the bourgeois society, hopes that Marxism, being a product of its environment, merely reflected. Even the idea that industrial production plays a role in the development of humanity was borrowed by Marx from bourgeois economists. Marxism may have been a reality and true at the time of the religion of science, of Darwin, of the steam engine and the textile industry, but now, when science has encountered relativity, uncertainty, and chance, electricity and atomic production, to maintain that truths a hundred years old are still valid is ridiculous and unscientific. "Marxism is only scientific today in defiance of Heisenberg, Bohr, Einstein, and all the greatest minds of our time."[10] Marx considered Darwinism the foundation of his method; to remain infallible then, Marxism must deny all discoveries in biology since Darwin; and the recent discoveries all introduce the idea of chance into biology, contrary to deterministic doctrines. Besides, Marxism was never scientific in the first place, for most of its major predictions concerning the future development of capitalism and of the working class and of the revolution never materialized. It was neither scientific nor consistent, and this is why it gave a false description of the future; it relied upon a "method ambiguous enough to wish to be simultaneously determinist and prophetic, dialectical and dogmatic."[11]

Finally, because today Marxism has adopted the bourgeois dream of uninterrupted development of production and taken this concept for an end in itself instead of a means for man's betterment, the result has been "the ruin of both bourgeois and revolutionary society to the benefit

of an idol that has the snout of power."[12] And now those
in power have called on Marxism—with its Utopianism
and its dream of an inevitable development toward a
better future—to justify all force and all methods to push
events into the predicted pattern.

In reply, Marxism similarly points to the bourgeois origin of the Existentialist philosophy and develops this attack in greater detail than does Existentialism. This is,
in many ways, Marxism's favorite and most damaging
form of criticism. Having established the roots of Existentialism in religion, a fact not difficult to demonstrate, the
Marxists turn to the discovery of the tie between ideas
or theories and the socio-economic condition in which
they appear.

Marxists state that Existentialism reflects the forlorn
position of the individual in the capitalist world; Existentialism developed when "the individual in the capitalist
world had not only been uprooted and cut off from the
social whole, but was also aware of himself as something
alien to this whole and even inimical to it."[13] In the Existentialist description of the non-true, commonplace life,
in which the individual is a thing rather than the real
man that he is, Marxists find the representation of human relations in bourgeois society that Marx outlined a
hundred years earlier. Existentialism, then, discloses the
crisis of bourgeois society, for it shows the incompatibility
between existing social relations and human freedom, and
also the individual's awareness of the hopelessness of the
situation.[14] This is nothing new; these are but expected
events:

It was Marx who first pointed out that in capitalist
society man becomes a thing and relationships between people are determined by those among things—
"the relations connecting the labor of one individual
with that of the rest appear not as direct social re-

lations between individuals at work, as what they really are, but material relations between persons and social relations between things." This is the crux of Marxian criticism of capitalist society. Marx rebelled against capitalism chiefly because capitalism crushed the personality and converted it into a thing. Yet Marx showed that the cause of this could be eliminated, and indicated the means to attain this end.[15]

Marxists realize that Existentialism does not recognize that the cause of man's alienation is the social structure of the capitalist society; Existentialism pretends to find the cause in man's consciousness. Therefore a change of social relations would have little or no effect upon man's "existential" alienation. Even under socialism or communism, in any society and at any time in history, such alienation is a real possibility. Only a change in consciousness, according to the Existentialists, will restore man to his true existence—transform him from a thing to an individual. But Existentialism does not want to recognize that man's consciousness is a product of social conditions; and it is because of this refusal that Existentialism sees the hopeless but courageous acceptance of reality as the only answer to the problem of man's existence. Sisyphus, in his condemnation to senseless and endless labor, is an excellent illustration of the condition of man under capitalism, and it is small wonder that Existentialism has chosen this myth of all others, as the one that best describes the Existentialist plight.

Georges Lukacs, the foremost Marxist critic of Existentialism, echoes these views and attempts an even more detailed examination of Existentialism, as a philosophy having its origins not only in bourgeois society, but in bourgeois thought as well. (It must be remembered that to show such an origin, is, for Marxism, a method of proving that a philosophy is historically reactionary and therefore false.[16])

Lukacs classifies Existentialism as the last attempt of bourgeois intellectuals to find a third way beyond materialism and bankrupt idealism, an attempt to remain in the realm of ideas and metaphysics in order not to be forced to face historical reality. It resembles earlier bourgeois philosophies in defining reality in terms of the subjective individual. And its distinguishing traits are irrationalism—as a method of escaping the rational confrontation of a culture condemned to extinction—and pessimism. Its view of history and of human reality is simply a "universalization of the plight of the bourgeoisie during the period of the decline of capitalism."[17] And given the historical situation, Lukacs predicts the continued rise of Existentialism as the dominant philosophy of bourgeois intellectuals.

The most interesting, and certainly the most humorous criticism of Existentialism is given by B. Dunham, an American Marxist, writing in the Soviet philosophical journal *Voprosy Filosofii*. First and foremost, he finds that Existentialists invariably fall into incomprehensible language when explaining their theories. Even Sartre, who has the gift of clarity when he wishes to make use of it, is at fault in this.[18] Quoting the fact that "Clarity is the God of the philosopher,"[19] Dunham poetically argues that under the light of clarity Existentialism would disappear as the shade before the sun. He agrees with A. J. Ayer that Existentialism is largely the art of misusing the verb "to be," and, for himself, adds that it makes an impression upon the minds of its readers through the use of such emotion-producing nouns as anguish, death, fear, care, guilt, despair, responsibility, engagement, commitment, alienation, and, especially, existence.

Dunham comments that every Existentialist denies that he is an Existentialist, which means only that he refuses to untangle the words of his colleagues. Existentialism is characterized by anarchy, especially the French

school which has as many branches as there are members.
And being an anarchical philosophy in practice it remains
true to form in its tenets:

> You think our theory is incomprehensible? Excellent,
> we never wished to make it comprehensible. It seems
> to you irrational? Even that is good: in irrationalism
> is found a higher wisdom. You think that among the
> various theories of Existentialists there exist sharp
> divergencies? Splendid, that is exactly what we de-
> sired. Our views appear to you unhealthy and not
> normal? Remarkable, health and normality are char-
> acteristic of primitive minds.[20]

What, asks Dunham, can one possibly do with people
who speak like this? Usually it is possible to take a philosophy, examine its beliefs, and criticize them, but with
Existentialism such a method is futile. He concludes that
Existentialism is not a philosophy but an illness, and it is
as an illness that he intends to examine and diagnose it.
He thinks that Existentialists are masochists, preoccu-
pied with their personal problems: the words they use
to describe the world do not describe the world but describe instead how they feel in the world—and they feel
badly. If a mature person has problems of the type that
the Existentialists seem to suffer from, he attempts to find
the cause and a remedy. But the Existentialists do not
want to be cured. In this passivity Dunham finds they
are like spoiled children. It is children, more than anyone else, who project their subjective wishes upon the
external world and interpret the world according to their
needs—whether it feeds, warms, and caresses them. They
come from the womb and desire the world to be like the
womb. The fact that the world is not like a womb is the
real psychological reason for the existential turning of
Berkeley's *"esse est percipere"* into *"esse est excruciare"*
—to exist is to be in agony—and the making of the new
axiom into their basic philosophical principle. Because of

this immature outlook on life, the Existentialists remind
Dunham of a screaming child in the hands of its mother.
And he adds, "please understand, that I in no way write
ironically. Inertia and passivity, the desire to spend the
entire life at the breast of the mother is characteristic of
all idealistic schools, and especially of Existentialism."[21]
Dunham concludes:

> Existentialists do not give us a description of the
> world or of man's place in the world, they only ex-
> press their infantilism which is raised to the level of
> a metaphysics. When Existentialists state that the
> world does not resemble the womb, they do not lie.
> But when they sorrow after the fact that the world
> does not resemble the womb, by this they announce
> that they as yet have not left and do not want to
> leave the mother's breast.[22]

A philosophy of tears and passivity cannot, of course,
propose any serious social theory, and in the end it becomes reactionary; its nihilistic tone is really a preparatory
course for fascism, a training for the acceptance and the
love of destruction and ruin. Only through his psychological analysis of Existentialism is Dunham able to explain
how a group of philosophers could arise in the middle
of the twentieth century, after three hundred years of
scientific progress, and condemn the hope that science
has given man, claiming that man is heading toward ruin
and agony.

Lukacs arrives at similar judgments in regard to Existentialism's social functions. He, too, states that Existentialism is not politically progressive but, on the contrary,
paves the way to fascism. (He admits Sartre has no
fascist tendencies, but argues that Sartre's progressive political views are incompatible with his Existentialist philosophy.) This lack of political progressivism is the result
of the philosophy's subjectivity and refusal to accept objective and scientific facts; indeed this is its greatest weak-

ness, for it cannot account for objective social historical forces, and so it cannot formulate a social philosophy. Existentialism is in spirit anti-scientific and anti-rational; it holds that the individual and his freedom can be safeguarded only in spite of science and reason, which are impersonal: "either individuality or science; either freedom or reason—such is the dilemma as posed by existentialism."[23]

These particular Marxist criticisms of Existentialism may be completed with a definition of Existentialism provided by the *Bolshaia Sovetskaia Entsiklopedia:*

> Existentialism: an ideological tendency of contemporary bourgeois philosophy. . . . Criticizing the one-sidedness of rational and mechanical understanding of the activities of man in society, Existentialism falls into even a greater one-sidedness. It is impossible not to notice in this philosophical doctrine a clear tendency towards irrationalism. From this stems the reactionary criticism of the scientific theory of the historical process developed by Marxism-Leninism. In an eclectic form, Existentialism attempts to unite the features of subjective and objective idealisms. The ideas of Existentialism are decorated with the sharp tones of a decaying, pessimistic world-view. The substitution of the category of essence with the category of existence leads Existentialism not to the surmounting of idealism but to the substitution of idealism with new shades and combinations of the old idealistic teachings.[24]

From the various statements above, it is evident that Marxists do not take seriously the Existentialist accusation that Marxism is anti-scientific or that it reflects bourgeois beliefs and attitudes. On principle, they consider such criticisms too farfetched and, rather than reply to them, they concentrate on disclosing Existentialism's connection with the capitalistic society and its openly anti-scientific, anti-rational, pessimistic, and nihilistic traits.

To a large extent, criticisms of the type reviewed above are possible only because of a deliberate and unsympathetic misunderstanding of the respective theories and positions. Nevertheless the criticisms, being general, are true in many cases and also in a general sense. It is undoubtedly true that Marxism has its roots in nineteenth-century bourgeois ideas and ideals of science and progress, that its claim to be scientific is vitiated by its prophetic and politically opportunistic spirit, that it was and is a response to working-class needs, that it holds an ambiguous concept of truth, that as a movement it does contain many trappings associated with religious sects, and that, again as a movement, it has a tendency to ignore the means it uses in order to force men into the predetermined world it has envisioned as the better, future society. Similarly it cannot be denied that Existentialism has its roots in religion and relies upon many religious concepts in interpreting man and the world, that it is in its basic tones subjective to an extreme, pessimistic, almost masochistic in some cases, irrational, anti-scientific, anti-historical, that particularly atheistic Existentialism is anarchistic and unable to construct a coherent social theory, or even to account for harmonious human relations, that some of its adherents were not exactly anti-fascist when Hitler was in power, and that, to a certain extent, it reflects the social conditions of Western man.[25]

In all these cases, however, a more thorough study would have to be made before the criticisms could be established as really characteristic of each school of thought, for all of them are subject to serious qualifications. To this extent they are merely generalizations, labels, and, in some cases, exercises in name-calling. Yet the similarity of criticisms by both camps reveals, interestingly enough, that Marxism and Existentialism have more in common than they perhaps realize. They both, for example, seem to favor the Greek world-view as opposed to the Judeo-Christian one, since they praise the former and criticize each other for having adopted the latter. Perhaps it is wishful thinking on both sides, but this implies that both desire to make peace with nature and society, that they are searching for harmony and beauty in the universe of nature and man. (On the side of Existentialism it is Camus, with his love of light, nature, and beauty to whom this applies particularly.) Next, they both consider science a value and a virtue, and feel that they have made a damaging criticism if they are able to show that some theory or fact is unscientific. (This applies to Sartre with qualifications, for he is prepared to criticize science as well.) They are also anti-religious and anti-bourgeois and gloat when they are able to find religious or bourgeois origins and ideas in each other's theories. In all these attitudes they are, more than either wishes to acknowledge, children of the age of science and of liberal, democratic humanitarianism, as exemplified by the ideals of the French Revolution. In this sense, Marxism as the earlier and the more developed philosophy may claim to have contributed a much greater share to the rise of these ideals, and even to have influenced Existentialism in some of its better traits.

chapter six

FREEDOM, ETHICS, AND ACTION

This chapter will discuss the interrelated matters of freedom, ethics, and action. Action will not receive separate attention, but will be dealt with by implication, at times overtly and at other times not so directly, within the framework of freedom and ethics. The topic is an extensive one, and it cannot be treated with justice in one chapter; however, a brief outline of the unique problems involved under this heading in the philosophies under discussion will be attempted.

Freedom

The first chapter of this book suggested strongly that because of the existential definition of man's consciousness as an emptiness, a "lack" with no essence, man *is* freedom. More than that, he is bound, chained to his freedom; he cannot escape it—except in death. By the nature of his consciousness, which is always in flux, always transcending itself, he is condemned to total, unconditional freedom. And Sartre gives no quarter in this; man "is completely and always free or he is not free at all."[1]

Practically, the fact that man is nothing but freedom means that he makes his essence, that he alone decides what he is, what he wants to be, what he wants to do—even by making no decisions in these matters, he has made one. And because he is free in this unqualified manner he is also totally responsible for everything that he decides, chooses, and does. Total freedom implies total responsibility, and total responsibility implies anguish and care. This last is particularly true because man must create his own values without any guides and without any reference to stable norms; he alone can give meaning to life and to all events that occur—past, present, and future. And in choosing, deciding, and acting for himself he also chooses, decides, and acts for others: "When we say that a man chooses himself, we do mean that every one of us must choose himself; but by that we also mean that in choosing for himself he chooses for all men."[2] Or again, "I am . . . responsible for myself and for all men, and I am creating a certain image of man as I would have him to be. In fashioning myself I fashion man."[3] These are examples of the all-encompassing freedom with which man legislates, and they are further causes of his care and anguish.

Freedom means choice, and if, in man, consciousness is freedom, then consciousness is also choice. "My choice is inseparable from my being and I am according to the way in which I choose myself."[4] Because man is condemned to freedom his choice is never final; at each moment as his consciousness grapples with new events, which it must structure and so define itself, he is in a position either to reject or to reaffirm his previous choices.

But are there really no limits to man's freedom? Apparently there are. Although there is no universal human essence, there are universal human conditions (supra, p. 12), and there are given situations in which a man finds himself and through which he must act: a pilot of an airplane is not free to leave the cockpit and go for a walk in New York's Central Park, nor is a poor man free to take a vacation trip to Tahiti. Therefore Sartre writes, "We do not do as we please, yet we are responsible for what we are: that is the brute fact."[5] Nevertheless, within a given situation man is still free to make of it and of himself whatever he will; and he must make something of it, given his nature. Yet this is somewhat of a paradox. It appears that "there is freedom only in a situation and there is a situation only through freedom."[6] The fact that man is condemned to be free is another limit and another paradox—he is a slave to his freedom, a freedom he is powerless to escape. The existence of others as free beings who by their "look" deprive a man of his total freedom to posit the world is another limitation. And, in the end, death is the final limit to man's freedom; but, again paradoxically, it is also the liberation from his freedom. The only other limits that man's freedom encounters are those that it places upon itself.

In the light of these limitations Sartre's statement that either man is completely free or not free at all seems overly strong. But these are common sense boundaries, or limitations of quite a different sort than those imposed on man by other world-views. And regardless of their effect, the result still remains that man is freedom and that in every situation he is able to do whatever he decides. This is where the emphasis falls.

The sad fact is that all freedom and all choosing are absurd; the entire phenomenon (like all life) is without any ground, without any reason, it just is—a naked, brutal, absurd fact of senseless existence. Because "the *en-soi* has no internal structure nor causal powers . . . . it cannot act nor be the *ground* of anything. Action seems to be restricted to man. In fact, the whole idea of a ground lacks any real basis beyond the processes of human freedom."[7] But human freedom can express itself only in "an arbitrary choice of some kind, which has no intelligible grounds. Hence in the last analysis, everything, both the *en-soi* which is simply there, and the *pour-soi* with its caprices, is ungrounded."[8] The only conclusion that can follow is that "everything is absurd. This he [Sartre] states as a truth that really holds of all being."[9]

Given this absurd abandonment of man and the conditions of his total freedom and total responsibility, it is no wonder that most men attempt to escape their freedom—the *real* situation of their and the world's existence.

They refuse to recognize the harsh reality and so they fall into bad faith (*mauvaise foi*) and self-deception. The end result of such bad faith is alienation. Through bad faith men become alienated from their true selves, and, in turn, from the world, from reality. Alienation takes the form of seeing ourselves as only a body, or a thing, or as the Other sees us, or as the role we play in society. It can also take the form of believing in absolute norms, or in unquestioningly accepting dogmas, customs, ideas. And finally, alienation can also be found in appropriation, in the identification of oneself with the objects one possesses. In all these cases of alienation a *spirit of seriousness* becomes evident, according to Sartre. The alienated man views his life and his role as a serious affair, nothing to be taken lightly, but something to which one must devote his being. Such a man is then estranged from his true self, and he is not free.

Marxists and materialists are examples of this *spirit of seriousness*, since their primary concern is changing or understanding the world. They attach more importance to the world than to man, and they give man being only in so far as he belongs to the world. "Seriousness in this sense . . . is the abdication of human presence in favor of the world, and the serious person buries his consciousness of his liberty at the bottom of himself."[10] "Marx," writes Sartre, "posed the chief dogma of seriousness when he affirmed the priority of the object over the subject, and man is serious when he takes himself for an object."[11]

In all the above instances of existential alienation the result is that the alienated man does not live an authentic existence but a false one: he sees himself as an object among objects and not as the free subject that he really is; his real *human* nature is hidden from him. John D. Wild's excellent book on Existentialism provides several descriptions of the unauthentic, slave-like existence opposed to that of the authentic, free existence.

In this world one does not commit himself beyond
the position [profession] that one tends to take. One
does not decide for himself, and shies away from
personal responsibility. . . . The exceptional is always leveled down towards the average. . . . One
is reassured by finding himself supported by widely
prevailing opinion. One tries to escape in a refuge
of nameless indecision from what is really and authentically his. This impersonal mode of existence is
unauthentic because deprived of personal freedom.
It is, however, an omnipresent fact. This is the world
to which we are all first introduced. If one is ever to
find himself, one must do so in the everyday world
of *das Man*.

At this stage of our history, the authentic person will
refuse to be lost in the world of public functions
without a struggle. He will try to understand his real
possibilities, and to make up his own mind in the
light of these. Aware of himself as a center of freedom, he will sharply distinguish between persons and
things. . . . He will wonder at things he does not
understand, and ask questions of himself and others.
Above all, he will not be afraid to stand alone.[12]

And there are other major differences. The unauthentic
man finds himself in a situation or falls into one; he solves
it only to discover that he is now faced with another
situation which also demands solution. His aim is to escape from the situation, and for this he finds science an
efficient instrument. The authentic person does not fall
into situations but brings himself into them:

He knows that in taking over his factuality, he has
committed himself to situationality as well. He is
aware that no escape is possible. . . . He has made
up his mind about what he is seeking. He knows
that it is *this* decision which has brought him to where

he is. . . . He does not postpone his decisions, because the structure of his world is clear. . . . Very
flexible in most affairs, on ultimate issues he is uncompromising.[13]

The unauthentic man, with recourse to fixed norms and
standards, attempts to escape his responsibility; the authentic man takes it upon himself. The unauthentic man
attempts to place his death away from his present situation: it is certain but not now. The authentic person accepts his death and permits the fact to influence his present decisions. The unauthentic person is not fully conscious
of his feelings and of the world he inhabits: he sees only
objective facts. The authentic person is deeply self-conscious: he knows that every object is given in a subjective way. The unauthentic person sees time and history as a succession of events which, once past, are over
and done with. The authentic person understands that
time and history are fluid, and he takes over the past and
looks into the future in all his decisions and actions:

> The authentic person realizes that he is not merely a
> set of events in history, but that his own existence is
> historical. He is skeptical of spatial metaphors, and
> doubts the theory of automatic progress. The past
> may factually determine, but its meaning is still un-
> certain. It is not so much a firm foundation for new
> achievement as a burden that presses upon us and
> restricts our field of action.[14]

And lastly:

> Freedom must not be confused with novelty. If this
> were its nature, freedom would be easy and auto-
> matic, for all that happens is novel. True freedom
> is hard and precious. It is open only to persons who
> have understood something of those final but still
> unfinished possibilities which here and there have
> brought meaning into the past. It is brought into be-

ing again at a present moment only by those who have decided between them with finality, and who exist with integrity up to the end.[15]

In other words, freedom is possible only for the person who leads an authentic existence.

It is clear from the above descriptions that the existential definition of freedom and its concomitant—authenticity—have little to do with the socio-economic situation in which a person finds himself. No determinism of any kind is acceptable: neither heredity, environment, economics, nor politics exercises a determining control over man's actions. He alone chooses their influence or rejects it. All motivation is inner. But regardless of time, place, society, or profession, or economic, social, political, educational, or cultural opportunities, most men are not free; they lead an unauthentic existence. And freedom is not won by a change of these environmental conditions, but by the recognition—in any situation—of one's real nature and authentic existence. It is an outcome of a change in consciousness. How such a change is achieved varies with every individual. In one it may be the experience of the world as a nausea-producing mass; in another, the sharp realization of man's mortality; and in still another, the rejection of all norms and the acceptance of total freedom and total responsibility.

Freedom as such may often be found in situations that by normal standards are considered opposed to the very idea of freedom. Here is Sartre writing after the war:

> We were never more free than during the German occupation. We had lost all our rights, beginning with the right to talk. Every day we were insulted to our faces and had to take it in silence. Under one pretext or another, as workers, Jews, or political prisoners, we were deported *en-masse*. Everywhere, on billboards, in the newspapers, on the screen, we encountered the revolting and insipid picture of our-

selves that our oppressors wanted us to accept. And, because of all this, we were free.[16]

Further on he adds:

At every instant we lived up to the full sense of this commonplace little phrase: "Man is mortal!" And the choice that each of us made of his life and of his being was an authentic choice because it was made face to face with death. . . .[17]

Such is the Existentialist definition of freedom and of a free existence.

These Existentialist attitudes toward freedom repel any Marxist. They are in fact incomprehensible to him. Indeed, in his article on Existentialism, B. Dunham (*vide* p. 93) quotes the above passage on freedom from Sartre as an example of the use of understandable words which in combination produce an impression of the densest and darkest of phrases: to speak of freedom under occupation! When Marxists examine Existentialist ontology and particularly the Existentialist description of the world and man's place in it, they find it even more difficult to understand where all this total freedom comes from and what it means in practice. For example, Adam Schaff asks how it is possible to have a completely free individual who "depends on his own decisions alone and at the same time [is] helpless and pathetically hopeless in his struggle against a malicious Fate."[18] To speak of freedom under such conditions is either ironic or incomprehensible. In contrast to the strange Existentialist conception of freedom, Schaff states that "Marxism shows that man, making decisions which are in a sense independent, and choosing a certain attitude or field of activity, always makes these decisions socially—in that his personal models are socially determined, that his foundations are, as Marx once said, a social product and that, from this standpoint, 'the individual belongs in fact to a definite form of society.' "[19]

In a recent book on Marxism and Existentialism, in which Schaff deals with this matter in detail, he gives the following possible definitions of freedom (excluding as unworthy of attention mechanical determinism and extreme voluntarism):

1. free is he who acts with a will which at its base is not determined by anything;
2. free is he who is not subject to any principles of historical development;
3. free is he who has the possibility of choice among one of many possible variants of actions.[20]

Schaff criticizes the more popular first two definitions and argues that the recognition of laws of historical development does not exclude but, on the contrary, forms the basis of man's creativity; that only upon objective social principles can realistically free actions take place. He therefore accepts the third proposition as the only one compatible with Marxism and affirms that this "conception of freedom refutes all philosophies of despair, theories of man as 'lonely,' 'condemned to choice,' 'living in anguish.' It is, despite its humbleness, a conception of faith in the power of man, in his social essence."[21]

Thus when Marxists speak of freedom they mean by this the ability of man to understand the laws of natural and social development and the possibility that such an understanding provides for man to shape these laws to his own ends and purposes. Herein lies the true and concrete conception of freedom. This is what is meant by freedom being the knowledge of necessity. It is only when facts and laws are not known that determinism operates and no freedom exists. Freedom is a choice based on an appraisal of an objective situation. Marxism is often criticized as a philosophy of *economic determinism;* the Existentialists, including Sartre, also lodge such criticisms against it. But this is not what Marx meant; there is no unfolding of economic forces with a mechanical relation to the course of social development, making ideas mere effects of basic economic causes. "This is *not* Marxism. What is at first an effect, the idea arising in a particular situation, immediately becomes itself a *cause*, and in fact, the really effective cause of social change."[22] Therefore it is not true that history follows a *fated* course; the Marxist prediction that a class will act in a certain way does not mean that it is determined in its activities and without freedom, but rather that if it wishes to survive it must act in the predicted manner. To illustrate this idea Marxists often use the analogy of the doctor who is certain that his patient will recover because he relies in his prognosis on the patient's desire to regain health and therefore on his responding to directions. "The Marxist holds that the victory of socialism is inevitable because he is counting on society responding to a certain program since it wishes to live."[23] Marxists do not hold that historical events are determined by some external necessity. "Events are determined by men and *ideas*, but these arise in certain historical circumstances and are only effective in so far as they fully reckon with them. Revolution is never automatic. Intelligent, resolute choice itself becomes the final historical factor which makes the revolutionary ideal come true."[24]

Here we have a description of what Marxists mean by freedom; it is based on reason, on reality, and, especially, on action. "The Hegelian freedom, and the cancelling out of alienation in the mind is not yet the reality. All this can only be attained by action."[25] Action toward what? Action directed toward the purpose of increasing every man's opportunity to a better and a fuller life—something that no individual can achieve alone, but that can be achieved only through the activity of the majority of individuals. Marxists are very concrete on what the goals of this freedom are—the end of economic exploitation, the granting of greater and better opportunities and benefits in economic, social, political, and cultural life to all men. In contrast, when the Existentialists speak of freedom what do they propose? The recognition of one's real nature and situation, both of which are subjective, malleable, but always absurd and therefore purposeless: absolute freedom in absolute absurdity? A strange freedom, to be sure. According to this definition, the worker and the slave can also be free any time they make an adjustment in their consciousness, in their understanding of the world. It is that abstract, idealistic freedom that Sartre inveighs against in his writings that he now proposes for all mankind. In practice, all that existential freedom offers man is a pessimistic outlook upon a senseless and hostile world, with no relief from this situation except in the so-called "self-deception" or in death. If a desire to change the world for the better is labeled disparagingly as a "spirit of seriousness," as alienation, and as "self-deception," something unworthy of the existentially free man, then what does Existentialism propose to do about the world's injustice, misery, and slavery of one type or another? Merely to recognize that they exist? What type of "spirit" is this? And what kind of freedom?

Existentialism did not invent the much-emphasized concept of alienation, which it shows to be the opposite of freedom. It was Marx who first gave a concrete definition of alienation—a historical phenomenon arising out of the division of labor and reaching its culmination and zenith in the capitalistic society, where man becomes an object, becomes identified with and ruled by the products he himself creates, and in so doing becomes estranged from his true nature, from his real consciousness, from his work, from others, and from society. Nor is the distinction between authentic and unauthentic existence original with Existentialism. It was again Marx who based the concept of alienation on the distinction between existence and essence, "on the fact that man's existence is alienated from his essence, that in reality he is not what he potentially is, or, to put it differently, that *he is not what he ought to be. . . .*"[26] And Marx went on to provide concrete, re-alistic rules for the removal of alienation and the conse-quent unauthentic existence. The Existentialist prescrip-tion for the removal of alienation and self-deception places man in a position certainly no better and very possibly much worse than the one he faced before. The Existential-ist recommendation seems to consist in saying: "Be a hero; grin and bear it."

The problem with Existentialism is its refusal to recog-nize that man's consciousness is the product of social con-ditions, that his actions are socially conditioned, and that therefore freedom or the lack of it is primarily a social fact and not only a matter of an individual's consciousness. Existentialism finds freedom not without but within man, and, accordingly, claims that a reorganization of social conditions does nothing to increase man's freedom: only a change in consciousness can do that. This, too, is an old theory, and Marx spoke of it when he dealt with certain adherents of Hegelianism: "This demand for changing man's consciousness reduces itself to a demand for inter-preting existence in a different way, which means recog-nizing it by giving it a different interpretation."[27] And, of course, a different interpretation and a recognition of pres-ent existence never brought about greater freedom for anyone, but it may have brought about a recognition of and a submission to slavery and exploitation. It is this kind of thinking that sees freedom at its zenith in the midst of a brutal military occupation of France. It is this kind of thinking that finds a perverse freedom in man's contem-plation of his own death. And it is this type of thinking that finds absolute, unrestricted freedom in a universe that it also describes as absolutely and unrestrictedly cha-otic, lawless, and absurd.

Finally, there are plenty of scientific proofs and psy-chological demonstrations that no man is free of his past, of his heredity, and of his environment, even if he wants to be or thinks that he is free of their guidance. It is not true that man alone makes himself what he is, that he alone bears the responsibility for his world, for his ideas and actions. No man lives alone; each man lives, acts, and thinks within a society, within a historical situation, within a given environment, and that environment, that society, and that situation mold him, his character, his ideas, and his actions. His responsibilities and his choices are movements shared by the entire structure in which he lives. All of this does not mean that he is an automaton, determined and therefore not responsible for himself and his deeds. It does mean that his freedom is not as unqualified, groundless, and absolute as the Existentialists like to say it is.

In the above exposition, the arguments concerning alienation begin to cross and miss their marks. The two philosophies speak of different things when they define alienation, but their definitions do not necessarily contradict each other. Marxists, with their dominant emphasis on economics as the source of alienation, cannot recognize validity in the Existentialist definition of alienation, which in principle is not determined or shaped by economic forces. It is true that the type of alienation and unauthentic existence described by Existentialism is a trans-historical occurrence, a matter of human consciousness, and as such capable of existing in any society at any time—including the prophesied classless society of communism. It is a manner of existing that characterizes most men regardless of their economic or other situation. While it may be true that certain societies contribute more to this type of existence than others, and that the existential authentic existence does little by itself to change injustice or economic deprivation, these factors have little to do with the validity of the description. Marxists with their definition of consciousness as a socially and class-formed entity leave little room for an interpretation of consciousness that is not based on concrete social causes. As they understand it, all alienation is a product of the economic environment and will be erased by a change in the economic structure. They expect the communist society to be free of alienation and of alienated men; yet if alienation, by their own acknowledgment, is the result of the division of labor, one wonders how it will disappear, unless they plan to do away with the division of labor required by an industrial society and return to primitive conditions.[28]

On the question of freedom Existentialism is vulnerable on numerous points, not all of them brought out by the Marxist position and arguments; most of these are internal problems, and Marxists seldom bother to dispute with a philosophy on its own grounds, even if at times it is to their advantage. Sartre writes that a free choice "is only an act of announcing projects and decisions already made by pure consciousness."[29] A commentator on Sartre remarks that if this is so then freedom is reduced to spontaneity and loses all meaning: man desires what he does and he does what he desires. Because of this conclusion Sartre must qualify his definition, which he does by demanding that a free act be "done with perfect lucidity, and that it involve an acceptance of responsibility for other men as well. If these conditions are fulfilled then the act is unconditionally free, value creative, and authentic or good."[30] The logical result of this is that *all* actions if they fulfill these criteria are free and good. (Such rampant subjectivism causes problems for Sartre when he begins to speak of ethics.) But even so, the demand that an action to be free must be undertaken in all lucidity, requires a constant tension in man which he is not able to sustain; this is why he has recourse to semi-conscious habits and to norms not always created by himself.

Serious doubts and problems must be also raised in connection with the Existentialist argument that there is no fundamental human nature, or human essence. The argument seems to say that at birth, and perhaps even more after reaching full self-consciousness, man is totally empty, a *tabula rasa,* for his consciousness is a nothingness, only a movement gravitating toward objects, and that therefore every man can make of himself what he will. But Existentialists would have to admit such extreme qualifications to this theory that the argument would no longer hold. First and foremost, a human being in his biological and psychological functions is still, and only, a human being, nothing else: he is not an ape, a dog, or any other living creature except man. It has been shown that there is a fairly identical organic and psychological structure in certain beings which causes them to sense, perceive, function, act, and think in a distinctive manner, a manner that characterizes them as human, as partaking of a specific human nature. This in itself establishes very important criteria and bases for human nature; and all beings who share these criteria are human—that is, men. Obviously the criteria are flexible, particularly since the human is characterized by its unstable and unfinished nature. Also, the criteria have to take into account innumerable particular and individual variations. If pressed, one could, in abstract theory, even admit of borderline cases where difficulties would be encountered in categorizing these cases as human. However, for practical purposes, human nature, purely as a biological and psychological manifestation, can be recognized and defined universally and is therefore universal. If Existentialism grants this much, and it is difficult to see how it could logically refuse, then what is its claim? What does it mean by saying that there is no universal human nature or essence? That no universal human God-given soul exists? But that is an altogether different matter. There does not have to be a soul in man in order to speak of a human nature; the physical basis is enough. And certainly Sartre is not arguing that men, if they so desire, can turn themselves into lower animals or something else; and even here the desire would probably be an expression of human nature, of human essence. Besides, does not Existentialism implicitly argue that there is a universal human nature when it defines *every* man's consciousness in the same manner, as an emptiness, and as a freedom, and as certain only of its own existence? Are these things not universal and common to all men?

Marxism has less of a problem on this issue, for it agrees to the universal physical and psychological human characteristics, but argues that the psychological ones particularly are extremely malleable and are shaped by a person's social environment.

Existentialism raises other issues in the area of freedom that require analysis. It appears that the authentic, existentially free man treats others as objects and therefore as means more than the unauthentic or self-deceived, unfree man does. The man who leads an unfree existence may engage in the practice of debasing other men to objects and means unconsciously, but the existentially free man does this consciously and therefore perhaps more thoroughly. This means, then, that *true* existential freedom is really "the debasement of others to mere tools by the rare man of character who has risen to the level of a richer, genuine existence, who has resolved in ruthless independence to fashion a life-toward-death, a freedom in finitude on his own pattern."[31]

And even if it is granted that in essence each man is free, how does one pass from this "essential" yet subjective individual freedom to objective universal political freedom? These are two different matters, related and yet not contingent: one does not necessarily follow from the other. Of what use is it to argue that in his essence every man is free and then to find that in practice this freedom of his is but an empty word? Unfortunately, given the Existentialist ontology such indeed is the case. Marjorie Grene, for example, asks how it is possible to reconcile the principle of mutual respect of free beings for one another's freedom with the existential principle that each man's freedom reciprocally implies the repression of every other freedom. And, quoting Sartre himself, she can only conclude with him that in Existentialism "respect for another's freedom is an empty phrase."[32] It is empty because it seems that one may be free even if the political order is a totalitarian one, and if the political order is a democratic one the personal ontological repression of others' freedom creates a society in which men still are not free. And then, as far as freedom is concerned, it makes little difference under what political system men live: as Sartre stated in "The Republic of Silence," sometimes they are more free under a tyranny.

In all these respects and in others treated in the preceding section, Marxism is justified in pointing out the emptiness of existential freedom. Nevertheless, Existentialism does reveal a limitation of Marxist freedom, which with its strong class and economic orientation misses the subjectivity inherent in the individual's experience of his own life and of the world in all its various aspects. The existential freedom is not as absolute as it may at times appear, for Existentialism does recognize that there are conditions and situations by which man's freedom is limited and through which it must express itself. Nor is Marxism as wholly deterministic as it may at times appear, for it recognizes the flexibility inherent in every situation in which actions take place. Marxism, however, grants the situation much more influence than does Existentialism. The Existentialists can say without reservations that man makes his own history; the Marxist must qualify this statement, in its usual meaning, almost out of existence. It is quite safe for Marxism to state that man makes his own history, for who else is there to make it; it is a tautology. But once certain restrictions are placed upon man's freedom in creating his own history, once history is viewed as a predominantly determined development that makes allowances for human choice in minor matters only, then man is still making his own history, yet certainly not as a free being. He is now something in between a free being and a machine responding to the laws governing its operations—a sort of elaborate IBM machine, which has a degree of operational independence. (It is little wonder that lately certain Marxists have become very much interested in cybernetics.) Existentialism, on the other hand, argues, and fairly successfully, for a more realistic freedom in man's daily activities and therefore in the creation of his own history.

Ethics

A possible Existentialist definition of man could state that he is an active, value-producing choice. His consciousness is defined as an absolutely empty nothingness characterized only by its activity, its gravitation toward objects. In this activity it gives meaning and value to all the objects it absorbs, and in so doing it is free to choose whatever meaning and whatever values it prefers. Thus, man is activity; man is freedom; man is choice. And being the bearer of all these functions at the same time, it is only normal that in him and through him they are all interrelated and dependent upon one another.

But bringing this abstract definition of man—specifically of his consciousness—to a more concrete level, what does Existentialism have to say about ethics? It has been mentioned above that because man is freedom and because there is no God, man is compelled to create his own ethics. There being no God, no absolute norms are possible, and therefore ethics are dialectical and relative. Existentialism specializes in pointing out situations in which all universal norms and values are inapplicable: situations where a conflict exists between two or more equally accepted norms.

Sartre provides an illustration of this type of conflict in "Existentialism Is a Humanism" by giving an account from his personal experience. A young man came to him during the Occupation of France to ask whether he should join the Resistance or remain at home to care for his senile mother. If he joined the Resistance and left his mother she would most certainly suffer and die, but he would at least have performed a service for his country. If he remained at home to care for his mother, then his nation would be deprived of his service, which could contribute perhaps greatly toward bringing about liberation. With either choice he was forced to perform some harm in one aspect for the good he would perform in another. And then there was the last problem, a problem that indicates the complexity of the situation in which man must act—if he were to join the Resistance and be killed on the same day, then his mother would have lost the aid of his services and his nation received no benefit from his decision.

It is under such conditions that man must act, and often he has no recourse but to choose one value to the disparagement of another; often, too, the situation is of a nature where some harm or evil may result from either choice, or where the outcome is indefinite. Existentialism contends that life, practical activity, is in most cases this ambiguous and complex, and it is in such ambiguity and complexity that man is asked to choose, to form his values. In other words, few actions can be wholly good (or wholly evil), for the repercussions of performing a particular action may produce much benefit as well as much harm, or may even be indifferent in results. But because man *must* act, and because all action involves a choice, man is condemned to create his own values, even though the situations he faces are ambiguous. And because this is the condition of his being—to act and to choose—he must also bear the responsibility for all his actions and for all his choices, again no matter what the results may be once their effect is felt in actual life. It must always be remembered that non-activity is also an activity and a choice, and the responsibility for the results of activity and non-activity is the same.

Sartre likes to compare ethics to art: both require creation and invention at each stage of the doing process. A man cannot decide *a priori* what should be done in every situation, as an artist cannot decide ahead of time what he will do once he begins to create. Thus ethics is a living, practical affair, never completed, constantly in flux, and never a simple choice between two radically opposed principles.

This is an outline of the basic ethical situation facing man at all times. It would be possible to stop here, but Existentialism is not satisfied with such a broad definition. It insists that in choosing, man always chooses that which is better, and not only better for himself but better for all. "What we choose is always better; and nothing can be better for us unless it is better for all."[33] In this sense, every man by deciding for himself decides for all mankind; and because of this, to act ethically he must always consider his action in the light of all humanity, as if by his action all other men could guide themselves and act in the same manner. Therefore his seemingly unlimited "liberty is far from being a solipsism, because the individual is defined only by his relations to the world and to other individuals. An authentic morality, then, will be one which takes into account the dual aspect of a man's existence as an individual and as a social being."[34] Still, because he can never find proof that he is the one to make such universal, ethical decisions, and because he can never be assured that his decisions are correct, he bears a great responsibility and with it great anguish and care. And, as was mentioned earlier, his responsibility is absolute—absolute in the sense of encompassing all of mankind, and absolute in the sense of answering for all that each man is and does, beginning with himself. Every man being totally free, every man is likewise totally responsible for all that he does; he cannot blame heredity, environment, passion, or anything else: a coward is a coward because he chose to be a coward, or because he did not choose to be anything else—period.

Once again it is possible to stop here, and end with a peculiar type of ethical relativism; however, Existentialism is still not satisfied and wishes to make matters even more concrete. Not all actions that are chosen are ethical since the choice may be mistaken, and although a mistaken choice may not be evil (or good) it is still a mistaken choice and, as such, not existentially ethical. On what grounds is a choice mistaken? On the grounds that the choice is performed in self-deception, in bad faith; it is then an unauthentic choice and therefore unethical, or rather amoral, for ethics can apply only to a true and unhindered choice, a choice which is possible only if man is conscious of his subjectivity and thus totally free. It is because Marxism makes man into an object that it does away with all ethics: "Dialectical materialism makes good and evil vanish conjointly, for it abolishes their source."[35] Only authentic existence is an ethical existence, and authentic existence means the recognition of one's freedom and, with it, the recognition that one's freedom is the foundation of all values. Freedom then is the value which has no end but itself:

> We will freedom for freedom's sake, in and through particular circumstances. And in thus willing freedom, we discover that it depends entirely upon the freedom of others and that the freedom of others depends upon our own. . . . I cannot make liberty my aim unless I make that of others equally my aim. . . . Thus in the name of that will to freedom which is implied in freedom itself, I can form judgements upon those who seek to hide from themselves the wholly voluntary nature of their existence and its complete freedom. Those who hide from this total freedom, in a guise of solemnity or with deterministic excuses, I shall call cowards. Others, who try to

show that their existence is necessary, when it is
merely an accident of the appearance of the human
race on earth—I shall call scum. But neither cowards
nor scum can be identified except upon the plane
of strict authenticity. Thus, although the content of
morality is variable, a certain form of this morality
is universal.[36]

Existential freedom, found only in authentic existence,
is the standard by which and *in* which all actions are
judged. And the conclusion is that every action is good if
it is performed in this existential freedom with respect for
the existential freedom of others, as the quotation above
indicates. The problem that such respect for the freedom
of others may be a contradiction in Existentialist ontology
has already been discussed, and does not preclude the
fact that ethically one may still strive to respect others'
freedom.

Simone de Beauvoir, Sartre's acknowledged ethical
theoretician, develops the existential ethic in greater detail. In her book, *The Ethics of Ambiguity,* she describes
two wrong ethical attitudes. One, that of infantile morality which openly accepts the authority and values already
created by society and guides itself by these, and the
other, that of the adventurer who is always indifferent
to the results of his actions upon others. She rejects both
of these as irresponsible. She argues that there are no
rules, formulas, or absolutes upon which man may rely
for guidance in conduct. All rules must come from within
each individual facing a particular situation in the
knowledge of himself as a free being; anarchy is avoided
because when man realizes that he is free he also realizes
that his freedom is in many ways dependent upon the
freedom of others for its existence. "Lest our cries be lost
in empty space I must have men near me who are ready
to hear me; and these men must be my peers."[37] A freedom enjoyed in solitude is an empty freedom and can-

not be considered freedom. However, a new choice does not have to be made at each moment and in each particular situation; once a general commitment is made toward a certain aim, then this general decision guides the actions in all situations that arise that have a bearing upon the aim. Lastly, the entire structure of activity, choice, and ethics remains ambiguous, for we are never certain that our actions will bring us to the desired ends; the world and life being basically absurd, we face a struggle that often leads to failure. However, the point is not to surrender; defeat should never be assumed from the start. Thus, an authentic existence, respect for the freedom of others, and a "stiff upper lip" are the three related aspects of what may be called *existential virtues*.

Given these ethical principles, when Sartre or De Beauvoir begin to criticize Marxism, the best they can do is to point out that a Marxist by his beliefs necessarily leads an unauthentic, self-deceptive existence, and that the Marxist theory is wrong because it denies man's subjective freedom and by so doing eliminates all ethics, including its own right to make ethical pronouncements. De Beauvoir, for example, comments that at one point Marxism seems to recognize man's subjective freedom, in his desire to transform and transcend an oppressive situation, but soon this subjective desire and will is absorbed into the objectively given world. "Revolt, need, hope, rejection, and desire are only the resultants of external forces. The psychology of behavior endeavors to explain this alchemy. It is known that that is the essential point on which existentialist ontology is opposed to dialectical materialism. We think that the meaning of the situation does not impose itself on the consciousness of a passive subject, that it surges up only by the disclosure which a free subject effects in his project."[38]

And De Beauvoir then proceeds to show that even with their determinism, and in contradiction to it, Marxists implicitly recognize man's subjective freedom. To believe in Marxism, to enroll in one party instead of another, to be active in it, to be indignant, or to admire, all these require a free and a subjective decision. Some Marxists might admit that such freedoms as listed here exist in action, but theoretically they condemn a philosophy of freedom. The same is true of their attitude toward morality; in practice they make moral judgments, but in theory they refuse again to acknowledge that morality is subjective and not an objective product of the material world.

Sartre's ethic, with all power given to the individual, who exercises this power in behalf of all mankind, has been characterized by one writer as a *heroic ethic*.[39] The same writer speaks of Sartre's description of human action as *historic action*, for it is entirely oriented toward the future. This has important connotations for ethics. "Sartre: 'Existentialism will never take man as an end, for man is always in a state of formation.' . . . De Beauvoir: 'It is in the light of the future, which is the meaning and very substance of the act, that a choice will become possible. . . .'"[40] And the consequences of this stress on the future are clearly described in De Beauvoir's statement that the "men of today will be sacrificed to those of tomorrow because the present appears as the 'facticity' that one must transcend toward freedom."[41] It now becomes clearer why Sartre can accept Marxism and Communism, for he finds them compatible with the Existentialist ethic.

Not all Existentialists agree with Sartre's position on ethics, particularly Albert Camus. This divergence on ethical principles between Camus and Sartre was the strongest contributing factor to their quarrel and separation. Simone de Beauvoir begins her book on ethics with the following quotation from Montaigne: "Life in itself is neither good nor evil, it is the place of good and evil, according to what you make it."[42] This already points out the radical difference between Camus and Sartre; Camus

would say that life in itself *is* good, and it can be made
better or worse. For if life is neither good nor evil then
it really does not matter much whether it is or not,
whether someone is killed or lives.

Camus very painstakingly rejects the heroism implicit
in Sartre's ethics and seeks to establish moderation and
limits: "'In order to be a man' one must 'refuse to be
God.'"[43] Camus is less interested in an anguished and
absolute choice of values in situations and more interested
in harmonious and pleasant participation with others
in life. Although not principles, these, too, are ethical
attitudes affecting one's behavior and values. Sartre is
more enamored of liberty, Camus of life. And because
life is now, Camus places a greater emphasis upon the
present. Sartre's orientation is to the future, for the present
is never there but is always on the wing. For Camus "no
appeal to the realm of ends, of the future, can justify any
attack on the present, on life which is an inalienable value.
Camus squarely sets up an ethic of being in opposition to
the ethics of action, and at this point he breaks with existentialism and Marxism."[44] But actually, in his emphasis
upon the present, Camus is more of an Existentialist than
Sartre. Camus is also more pessimistic than Sartre concerning a progressive future. In the case of ethics Sartre
must rely upon the future and hope that it will produce
good results, even though he knows that no matter what
the future will be like it can never vindicate his original
choice. In Sartre the existential conditions of the choice
in the end override the results; for Camus it is the results,
and always only the present results, that determine the
choice.

Camus, too, has an ethic of ambiguity, somewhat different from Sartre's, but equally as vibrant: "Horror and injustice exist within our own selves, in others, and in the
world. Thus in a simultaneous 'yes' and 'no' Camus defines
a dialectic of confrontation, of opposition, of anguish without transcendence. Camus's well-known 'concept of limi-

tations' simply means that an affirmation of life must be made which does not end in a complete negation of the world."[45]

Camus therefore is in a stronger position than Sartre in the ethical attack on Marxism. Sartre can argue only that Marxism is amoral; Camus can claim that it is immoral. And his claim is based on the argument that human life is the primary and the final value. Once human life is considered as part of a historical development, which supposedly aims toward a better life, then all murders can be justified. It is against this misuse of ideas, power, and man that Camus rebels. Here is his condemnation of Marxism:

> The aims, the prophecies are generous and universal, but the doctrine is restrictive, and the reduction of every value to historical terms leads to the direst of consequences. Marx thought that the ends of history, at least, would prove to be moral and rational. That was his Utopia. But Utopia, at least in the form he knew it, is destined to serve cynicism, of which he wanted no part. Marx destroys all transcendence, then carries out, by himself, the transition from fact to duty. But this concept of duty has no other origin but fact. The demand for justice ends in injustice if it is not primarily based on an ethical justification of justice; without this, crime itself one day becomes a duty. When good and evil are reintegrated in time and confused with events, nothing is any longer good or bad, but only either premature or out of date. Who will decide on the opportunity, if not the opportunist? Later, say the disciples, you shall judge. But the victims will not be there to judge. For the victim, the present is the only value, rebellion the only action. Messianism, in order to exist, must construct a defense against the victims. It is possible that Marx did not want this, but in this lies his responsibility which must be examined, that he incurred by justifying, in

the name of the revolution, the henceforth bloody struggle against all forms of rebellion.[46]

And it is a constant, ceaseless rebellion that Camus is advocating, a rebellion of both a "yes" and a "no," which affirms the present but rejects its injustices, and which struggles against the injustices always in the present, never postponing the day of judgment to the future. These are the differences between a revolution and a rebellion. The rebellion announced by Camus functions before, during, and after the revolution. The revolution exists only for the moment: before is a time of preparation and after a time of adjustment. Before and during the revolution all values are determined by its success. But what happens after the revolution is successful? Will justice prevail and will all other revolutions be forbidden? This is the question Camus poses to revolutionaries; and he greatly doubts that a Utopia will ever be achieved. Therefore his solution is a perpetual watch over injustice, with the highest value placed on human life. In some ways he speaks in the manner of Trotsky's "perpetual revolution" or of Marx's "beyond communism."

As in the matter of materialism and consciousness, so in ethics Marxism agrees with Existentialism on the most fundamental principles: the world is matter; there is no universal human essence; and there are no universal or absolute ethical norms. But as in the previous cases, the fundamental agreement is soon lost to sight when each philosophy begins to develop its particular theories. Marx never developed a systematic ethical theory, especially one dealing with individual moral problems, but considered the question one that would solve itself, given the premises of his theory that history is inevitably developing toward a more "human" order. In his and in Engels' writings three types of moral views are found: there are no universal moral standards, but all morals are established by classes, with different moral laws for different classes according to their economic and social interests; the moral values which will be in the future are superior to those of the present; and, a view not explicitly stated but implied, that a "really human" morality[47] exists which is trans-historical and therefore not relative.

It has been Marx's followers, beginning with Leon Trotsky (*Their Morals and Ours*), who have been compelled to deal with ethics in a more concrete and thorough fashion. The theory as it stands today is well exemplified in the views of the French Communist R. Garaudy. Writing for the Soviet journal *Voprosy Filosofii*, Garaudy rejects all contemporary ethical systems—Existentialism, Catholicism, Positivism—as inadequate and unrealistic, and raises Marxism as the standard for ethics. He finds economic alienation the key to all moral problems, and the overcoming of this alienation the goal of true morality. He argues that the overcoming of alienation is possible only at this time in history, when alienation has become an all-encompassing social fact. Freedom from alienation in the capitalistic society is not a concern of one class only, but of all men; for under capitalism even the wealthy become alienated. However, only the working class is in a position to accomplish the feat of liberating all men, since other classes still reflect the old, partial reality and consequently hold a false morality that is unrealistic and restricting. Because of this, the proletariat has a moral superiority over all other classes:

> Marx with his discovery of the laws of development of capitalistic society, of its inner dialectic, demonstrated that only the struggle of the working class permits the overcoming of alienation, that is the dehumanization of man. Therefore the first commandment of Marxist morality consists in this: to participate with all strength in the struggle of the prole-

tarian whose class assignment is identical with the liberation of all mankind.[48]

In this struggle every man is able to find his own deepest personal goals, for only in so taking part can he aid the full realization of humanistic principles, of true human freedom. And making a thrust at Sartre, Garaudy comments that this Marxist freedom does not come from nothing, but on the contrary is born in being, in real life:[49]

In this manner, Marxist morality returns to man all power, but with it also all responsibility, which left him with religious alienation. It is necessary to make man understand, says Maxim Gorky, that he is the creator and the master of the world, that upon him falls the responsibility of all evil on the earth, but that to him also belongs glory for all the bounties of life.[50]

As an aside, it must be noted that Gorky's words are very reminiscent of the Existentialist description of ethics, and are somewhat at odds with strict Marxist theory as regards man's role and responsibility in history.

Beginning his attack on every idealistic morality, Garaudy, in another journal, quotes Marx as stating that for true humanism there is no greater enemy "than spiritualism or speculative idealism which substitutes for real man 'consciousness of himself' or 'the soul.'"[51] And Garaudy continues, "if one underestimates the material conditions of the life of man, one does not change the world, but only the idea which men have made of it."[52] Such a morality, he claims, always pleases the bourgeoisie because in this way it loses nothing of its class privileges.

Reverting more specifically to French atheistic Existentialism, Garaudy states that it is incapable of establishing a morality for two reasons:

1. Sartre's conception of the Other, which speaks of absolutely free individuals whose contact with each other

causes only conflict through a reciprocal limitation of one another's freedom. "Idealism has always become transformed into solipsism," adds Garaudy.

2. Sartre's conception of Freedom, which is a freedom based on nothingness and capable only of negation, of saying "no," never of doing something constructive.[53]

Under such conditions the individual is incapable of a harmonious life with others, and of effective activity in history; this leads only to absolute moral nihilism.

Another article in *Voprosy Filosofii* by a Soviet writer also takes Sartre's ethics to task. The author repeats the usual Marxist criticism that Existentialism is a product of the crisis of capitalist society. Existentialism describes the ethics and the freedom of the lonely, closed individual whose only hope is in his own strength, who is alienated from the rest of society, and whose economic freedom is accompanied by fear. Existential freedom and ethics appeal to the bourgeoisie because in reality they argue for the passive acceptance of situations over which one has no power. Sartre's argument about the relationship between man's goals and means, described in *Being and Nothingness,* is revealing in this sense. Sartre argues that we encounter certain obstacles only because we choose certain goals; if the goal is changed the obstacle disappears. Thus for a mountain climber obstacles appear because he chose to climb the mountain; if he does not wish to overcome the obstacle he can always choose to climb another mountain or do something else. The Marxist writer, K. A. Schwartzman, comments that this may be a position applicable to mountain climbing, although no decent alpinist would agree, but in the basic necessities of life such a view leads to absurdities: to live man must work, but if he cannot obtain work in a capitalistic society, then he should change his goal—perhaps decide not to live, and so kill himself.

Schwartzman criticizes Sartre's idea that man is absolutely free in positing moral norms, as if each man were

not bound and restricted in his moral decisions by the social environment, by history, by his class outlook. Sartre
can argue in this fashion because he does not recognize
that there are social laws and influences that guide man
in his morality as well as in his other activities. Sartre is
correct in calling his ethics ambiguous because he rejects
all objective social criteria and gives man an abstract, free
moral choice; such an ethic can produce only ambiguity.
Schwartzman wants to know how Sartre can speak of
moral and social responsibility if he divorces every individual from others and from society. Moral action and criteria can be found only in concrete social life, not in an
abstract sphere of nothingness. The example of the artist
used by Sartre to demonstrate existential ethics is false,
for the analogy ignores the fact that the artist is influenced by his environment; he is not free of it. On the contrary, the better the artist, the better he reflects the surrounding reality. The same is true in ethics.

Existentialism's only criterion for moral actions is that
they be chosen in a fully free, conscious manner: this
would mean that "the appearance of bravery in battle
or desertion from the field of battle are equivalent, so long
as one and the other are the result of a free choice."[54]
With such a criterion no value judgments can be made,
and the result is total amoralism; in practical life this
means the toleration and defense of social evil. The character of the choice is important, not the goal, as if social
betterment is not and could not be made a criterion and
an aim for man's actions and a basis for value judgments.
The Existentialist criticism of Marxism as amoral because
of its determinism is not valid; Marxist determinism does
not stop all choice and ability to make value judgments
and criticisms. Schwartzman quotes Lenin: "the idea of
determinism, establishing the inevitability of human activities and rejecting the silly little story about free will,
in no way destroys either the reason, or the conscience of
man, or the evaluation of his deeds. Completely to the

contrary, only with a deterministic outlook is a strict and correct evaluation possible, and not the unloading of anything at all upon the free will."[55]

By claiming that the antagonistic social relations peculiar to capitalistic society are true for all societies, and by emphasizing the lone, alienated individual as the ideal, Existentialism in its ethics is anti-humanistic and nihilistic, because it *a priori* rejects the struggle for a better society and for better human relations:

> And so, in words, Existentialists declare the dignity of the human person. But in practice Existentialist ethics lead to the rejection of the authentic humanity in man and to a reconciliation with anti-humanistic relations which are characteristic of bourgeois society and expressed in the formula "man for man is a wolf," and even to the rejection of life itself, to the praise of death.[56]

Not all Marxists take a totally critical attitude toward Existentialism and the ethical questions it raises. Adam Schaff, mentioned in this connection earlier (*supra,* p. 106), for example, finds in Existentialism fruitful problems that he thinks deserve solving from the Marxist point of view, problems that he feels Marxism has neglected for too long a time. He lists these as, "(a) personal responsibility for one's own actions, also in the field of politics, particularly in situations involving a conflict of various moral principles; (b) the place and role of the individual in the world; this latter issue is rather vaguely and nebulously described as the problems of the 'meaning of life.'"[57] He posed these problems in a short article in 1959, and in 1962 a book was published in Polish dealing extensively with these and other matters related to Marxism and Existentialism. According to the Soviet review of this book, Schaff argues that not all responsibility is moral —as Existentialism claims—but that there are clearly defined responsibilities of a legal and a political character.

Moral responsibility comes into play in situations where no legal sanctions apply or in situations that pose morally conflicting issues. Here the responsibility is moral but the individual choice is still influenced by the social conditions, for man in his makeup is always an "ensemble of social relations."[58] True responsibility for one's actions is feasible only with a conception of the universe and of social life as a predictable and a caused process, for then man is able to see what the result of his actions will be. Both of these ideas, that the individual is necessarily influenced by his environment and that history and society develop according to predictable laws, are denied by Existentialism, making its ethical theory unrealistic and even nihilistic. In contrast, Marxism maintains that when man chooses he does not choose in a vacuum, that his criterion for the choice is not his own egocentric desire, which inevitably conflicts with the desire of others, but that he is guided in his choices by the solidarity, the unity, and the needs of his class and of his society. As for the "meaning of life," Schaff finds that to ask about the meaning of life is to ask about the purpose of life. And if life has a purpose —and for Marxists with their goal of a humanistic society it does—then life has a meaning. Because Existentialists cannot find a purpose in life, which they describe as an absurd accident incapable of being anything else but absurd at all times, they cannot find a meaning in life; they find more meaning in death.

Both Marxists and Existentialists clearly see that the root of their disagreement on ethics, as on many other matters, is in the different conceptions they hold of the individual and his consciousness.

The Marxist reply to Existentialism given directly above is fully applicable to Sartre's position and successfully repulses his criticisms; but it does not adequately cover Camus' criticism. He is difficult to deal with. His ethics are similar to those of the Polish writer Kolakowski, who

would defend the "intellectual attitude" of doing nothing
if the only possible action is to murder. Both do not dis-
claim violence, but simply refuse to make it a policy. The
accusation then follows that they refuse to get their hands
muddy and let others do the dirty work for them. And it
is explained to them that one cannot make an omelet
without cracking eggs, and that it is better that few die
now than many later. Camus and Kolakowski seriously
question the validity and particularly the morality of these
arguments and the truth of the prophecy or the assumption concerning the better future; the present is their concern, and it is to the present that they wish to apply
ethics. This is how the Intellectual speaks in one of
Kolakowski's essays: "If you represent a specific historical
reality, on what basis do you ask me to affirm it morally
merely because it is a reality? I will not support any form
of historical reality solely because somebody persuades
me that it is inevitable, even if I believe in its inevitability,
for which, by the way, I have no evidence. If crime is the
law of history, then does my awareness of this law suffice
to make me a criminal?"[59] Marxists with their certainty
concerning the laws of social development, laws that cul-
minate in the "good society," could not accept such passive and even restricting ethics; a passive ethic for them is
immoral, for it defends the oppressive status quo and
does nothing to bring about the better conditions predicted for the future. This view, plus the Marxist moral
criterion that everything that aids the proletarian struggle to victory is good and everything that hinders it is bad
—in other words, that any means may be used to attain
the desired end, with the end justifying the means—establishes Camus' ethical criticism of Marxism as correct.
Marxism is only too willing to sacrifice present lives for
those of the future.

Nor does Marxism adequately reply to the charge that
a deterministic philosophy cannot account for moral value
judgments. Lenin says that this is not so; Schaff argues

that some choice still exists in the given situation, but neither can deny what Marx wrote: "My standpoint, from which the evolution of the economic formation of society is viewed as a process of natural history, can less than any other make the individual responsible for relations whose creature he socially remains, however much he may subjectively raise himself above them."[60] And other problems arise, given even a smaller amount of Marxist determinism, which is what present-day Marxists seem to be arguing for: if morality is relative and a product of a given historical period and society, why do the identical moral problems seem to arise at all times and in all societies and equally concern all classes; and how does one know what is objectively inevitable and what is subjective, what is the main historical trend and what is an accident? This last problem is an interesting one and deserves illustration:

. . . Let us suppose that I agree with Marx's theory; suppose I agree that history proceeds by inevitable stages to a utopian end; suppose I agree that all morality is class-morality and therefore relative, and suppose I choose to adopt the morality of the proletarian class since it is the morality of the future and in some ways superior to the morality of the past. Suppose I agree and adopt all these views; what then do I do in the case of Stalin. Here we have a man who is educated in socialism, who spent his entire life dedicated to its cause, who represents the vanguard of the proletarian class, who is the leader of a mighty socialist society. His entire consciousness—thoughts and actions—are shaped and formed by socialist ideas and socialist surroundings. And what is the result of this socialist upbringing; what is the product of this socialist society? He lies; he kills innocent people; under false pretexts he even murders some of the most prominent members of the socialist revolution in Russia. In general, he is a merciless despot and an abso-

lute tyrant. I live under Stalin; I am one of his co-
workers. His methods repel me; I see his "errors and
excesses." He assigns to me tasks which I cannot reconcile either with my conscience or with my idea of
what is beneficial for the working class and for the
future society. What do I do? Didn't Marx say that
historical periods and events produce the men
needed for the tasks of that period. Is not Stalin's
rule therefore inevitable, and if inevitable is it not
also true and good and right. I do have an alternative:
I can withdraw from political life. But what if I don't
want to do that; what if I want to participate in history, if I want to aid its development. My only choice
then becomes to obey Stalin, to aid his designs, to
act perhaps even more ruthlessly than he, for then I
am really bringing Communism sooner to the earth.
Here the argument begins to turn nonsensical.[61]

The argument holds for other tyrants of history; and
even if it is argued that Stalin or several of the others were
accidents (Plekhanov acknowledges historical accidents),
the moral problem of the individual involved does not
disappear, or change for the better. On the contrary, it
becomes more complicated, for then one has to decide
whether to support or oppose the accident, especially if
such an accident lasts a lifetime and if it is not totally off
the predicted course of history, as in the case of Stalin.
There is no escaping the fact that Existentialism points to
a realistic problem when it insists that ethics are a subjective and primarily individual affair and are void if the
individual is an object moved in his decisions by a determined world.

However, Existentialism has faults of its own, many of
them clearly brought out in the Marxist counterarguments. It is true, for example, that Sartre does argue that
obstacles can be removed by a change of goals, and therefore Schwartzman's criticism of this proposition when

applied to practical life is correct. It is also true that Existentialism sanctifies almost every action so long as it is performed in the consciousness of one's freedom. Thus getting drunk at a bar is ethically as valuable as running the affairs of government, so long as both actions are chosen in freedom. In this sense Sartre's criticism of Marxism and Marxists as manifestations of the "spirit of seriousness" becomes greatly qualified, for if a person consciously and freely adopts Marxism, as in the case of Sartre perhaps, then the actions one performs as a Marxist are authentic. In the same manner, what if a person freely accepts De Beauvoir's infantile morality or the morality of the adventurer (*supra,* p. 120); does such morality then become authentic and therefore ethically good? What is to prevent one from freely adopting one system of ethics instead of another? According to Existentialism, all unauthentic actions are amoral, and all authentic actions are moral, with the broad, undefined, and contradictory reservation that one respect the freedom of others. Immoral actions seem to be lost, unless all unauthentic actions are judged as immoral, or unless Existentialists reserve for themselves the right to judge which actions are moral and which immoral. A strange and a thoroughly confused ethical theory—truly ambiguous. And this is not all. Why does it necessarily follow that total freedom implies total responsibility, given that both may be *total*? The two are not contiguous unless one wishes to make them so, that is, unless one makes an initial moral assumption or decision that they be related. For it is a moral decision. It is quite possible to have total freedom and simply reject all responsibility, or perhaps argue that responsibility is a restriction on total freedom. And if this is accomplished in the consciousness of oneself as totally free, then the action is authentic and therefore moral. And yet a further point—Sartre states that a person *always* chooses that which is better for himself and at the same time better for all. Again, the one does not follow from the other. What one person chooses may be better for him but not for others, and even less for all. True, in choosing one should choose as if the entire world were watching and as if all men were to make the same choice. But why assume that this will be so, that a man will choose with the rest of mankind in mind, or that he will not be selfish, irresponsible, or that he will not make serious mistakes in his decisions?

And lastly, it is worth considering whether the unauthentic existence of man, which is an attempt to overcome the unbridgeable gulf between the in-itself and the for-itself, is not more conducive to individual respect, love, social harmony, and effectiveness in action, than the authentic existence, which creates only conflict and consciously sees man as a means and not an end. The more authentic a man is the more isolated he becomes. It may be that the best course and the most moral course of action would be the rejection of the authentic existence and the cultivation of the unauthentic existence—somewhat in the style of the Grand Inquisitor and his priests. The objection would be that the truth is better than falsehood, under all circumstances, regardless of how much harm it does to the individual or to the society. But this, too, becomes a moot question and a moral one as well, full of ambiguity and one to which no *a priori* answer can be given.

chapter seven

THE UNION OF MARXISM
AND EXISTENTIALISM

Herbert Marcuse writes that the problem for philosophy after Hegel was to answer the question of who would fulfill the essence of man and who would realize philosophy.[1] He observes that two distinct philosophical branches appeared, each with its own reply; one, that of Feuerbach and Kierkegaard, who stressed the individual; and the other, that of Marx, who stressed the society. This, from the beginning to the present day, is the basic difference between Marxism and Existentialism. These philosophies are both direct descendants of Hegel, but with the mystical and absolute elements removed.

The Existentialist description of the individual's consciousness as always in flux, as a nothingness, owes its origin to Hegel's analysis of the third stage of consciousness, the Unhappy Conciousness, in *The Phenomenology of Mind*. There Hegel speaks of consciousness as "neither more nor less than an absolutely fortuitous imbroglio, the giddy whirl of a perpetually self-creating disorder. . . . for it is the negativity of all singleness and all difference."[2] This corresponds exactly to the existential description of consciousness as a "lack" and as a great wind gravitating toward objects with the power of negating them. The difference, of course, is that Hegel proceeds to a fourth stage of consciousness in which the union between the consciousness and the universe is attained, that union of the *pour-soi* with the *en-soi* which for atheistic Existentialism is an impossibility. Existentialism remains at the third stage and refuses to recognize any Absolute Spirit that would permit such a union. And so, in the words of one commentator, the Unhappy Consciousness is one that is "moving desperately and uncertainly between these two realms, repeatedly falling short of the perfection which it had placed above it in the heavens, [and] the free mind is tortured."[3] These are words that parallel Sartre's when he writes about the ceaseless but frustrated effort of man to unite the *pour-soi* and the *en-soi*, and concludes that man is a useless passion.

Marx, too, owes a great deal to Hegel, and he is much more frank than the Existentialists about his debts to the philosopher. It could be said that Sartre did to Hegel in epistemology and ontology what Marx did to Hegel in cosmology and history. That is, they both turned him on his head, or rather off his head and on his feet by retaining his ideas but placing them in an empirical context; they replaced the Spirit by matter, and the reason of the world by the reason of man.

Thus they are brothers but with opposing traits: one describing only the individual and the other describing only the society; one beginning from the interiority of consciousness and the other from something external to consciousness; one unable to account for a social theory and the other unable to account for the subjective individual; one much too subjective and the other much too objective. Sartre realizes this complementary opposition and thinks that if a union of the two could be achieved a splendid theory would result. He admits that Existentialism cannot provide a social philosophy and that Marxism is the only philosophy that is viable in this respect; but he thinks that Existentialism is true in its conception of the individual and of his consciousness.

This was the gist of his argument in "Question de Methode" (or "Marxism and Existentialism"), an earlier essay that now appears as the introduction to *Critique de la Raison Dialectique,* where he stated: "We are at the same time deeply convinced that historical materialism provides the only valid interpretation of human history and that Existentialism constitutes the only concrete approach to reality."[4] This would mean that Marxism is true in the sphere of practical social action, but that it is not based upon realistic and true philosophical principles. And therefore Sartre writes: "How has it happened that we are not simply Marxists? It has happened because in the statements quoted above [Sartre had quoted from Garaudy and Engels] we see suggestions for actions, statements of tasks and problems, and not concrete truths. . . ."[5] And he proceeds to argue that unfortunately Marxism, for the sake of political unity, has become dogmatic, tautological, and is no longer dialectical, and that consequently it turns the individual into an object. He therefore envisions his own task as follows:

This particular [present-day] Marxism presents Existentialism with its most important problem: to work out a theoretical foundation which would permit, without falling into the mystification of liberalism, the stabilization of the status of the individual in a socialistic society. This is how our practical and our theoretical tasks coincide: a concrete and positive theory of the real person which indicates the specificity and unmanageability of human existence to economic categories, and in general contrasting human existence to things and ideas, can aid in the democratization movement in the same way that the idealism of Stalinism theoretically and provisionally justified terror. Man the creator and recreator of his own and all human life, the creator of meaning and values, the only factor actively managing history, unceasingly conquering an existing situation to his objectivization, is man's future, as well as his immediate present. Man is man's problem, but he is also his neighbor and brother.[6]

Sartre continues further along these lines and states that it is his hope that the problem of restoring "man to his rightful dimensions"[7] is only provisional, since it is not Marxism, he claims, which has repulsed Existentialism, but only certain Marxists who are victims or associates of Stalinist reality. And he thinks that this factual but not ideological border separating the two philosophies will soon be overcome, with the democratization of the socialist countries and their acceptance of scientific disciplines so far rejected, such as psychoanalysis, sociology, etc., and with their use of the dialectical principle in the formation of new theories:

> When socialistic man finally appears in a closely conditioned history, as his synthetic project, which projects itself towards its own objectification, conquering and preserving in unity of work and action various structures describing him, when the history of mankind reveals itself in all its richness, that is, in the total of its meaning, then Marxism will again become the philosophy of our time and existentialism will lose the reason for its existence. For the time being, caution will do no harm; we must for some time tend our ideological garden ourselves. The absurd contradictions of these two thoughts actually forming one brings but one benefit; it will favor—even if by debates, discussions, criticisms, and reservations which will be evoked from both sides—the thawing of minds.[8]

And so, Sartre is saying to the Marxists, "Look, you have what we need—a practical theory of society, and we have what you need—a realistic theory of the individual; let us therefore unite." However, the Marxists want no part of the proposition. They continuously explain to Sartre that they appreciate his interest in Marxism, but that they would appreciate even more his decision to be either a

Marxist or an Existentialist. They constantly point out to him that the two are contradictory and incompatible. In commenting upon Sartre's stand as he has outlined it in "*Question de Methode*," this is what the foremost Polish Marxist, Adam Schaff, has to say about Sartre's views:

> Between the Sartre who remains loyal to Existentialist tradition and the Sartre who accepts the philosophical position of Marxism there is a contradiction that can only be overcome through the repudiation of one of the antagonistic positions now observed in his views. In its most concentrated form this contradiction is noticeable in the treatment of the problem of the individual.[9]

And then he proceeds to quote Marx's definition of the individual and his consciousness and contrasts it with the existential definition. In reply to Sartre's proposal for Existentialism to fill the Marxist gap on the individual and then to cease its existence, Schaff has the following to say:

> Everything depends on how we interpret this statement. If it implies "supplementing" Marxism with Existentialist theory and method, the whole proposition is pointless, since fire cannot be supplemented by water. If, on the other hand, what Sartre means is that the problems of man—which for different reasons have been, historically, monopolized by Existentialism—should be tackled by Marxism and on the basis of Marxist method, this is an important proposition deserving a most careful and penetrating analysis.[10]

And it is this analysis that has occupied Schaff in his later work.

The Attempted Union

Sartre, too, did not remain idle after the publication of the above essay in the fall of 1957, and in the years that followed he devoted much time to his proposed formulation of a philosophical synthesis of Marxism and Existentialism. The result of his labor was the cumbersome and difficult *Critique de la Raison Dialectique* published in 1961.[11]

In *Critique de la Raison Dialectique* we find a completely different Sartre from the Sartre in *Being and Nothingness*. In the latter work Sartre was interested in individual ontology and psychology to the exclusion of almost everything else. It was this one-sided but masterly emphasis that made him the dominant spokesman for French atheistic Existentialism. *Being and Nothingness* was the book of a young man—vigorous, uncompromising, and abstract. In the *Critique* Sartre deals primarily with sociology and with a psychological examination of social groupings and institutions. The emphasis upon the individual and the individual's psychology is gone. The *Critique* is the book of an older man—cautious, qualified, and realistic. The Marxist or purely logical and philosophical arguments brought against Sartre's Existentialist position in the previous pages of this book are no longer applicable when confronted with many of his new views in the *Critique*. This is so because Sartre has implicitly renounced his former ideas concerning the individual and his relation to society and has adopted many of the basic principles of Marxism. Nevertheless, Sartre is still Sartre, and his approach to Marxism is through a modification of his earlier theories. Vestiges of his Existentialist categories and concepts remain, and these are still vulnerable from both the Marxist and the purely philosophical points of view.

The title of Sartre's book indicates that he wishes to undertake a critique of dialectical reasoning. Yet the book is more of a critique of the lack of dialectical reasoning on the part of present-day Marxists. Furthermore, it is less of a critique, in the strict sense of the word, and more of a *development* of the very general Marxist idea of the dialectic into a more precise and more defined method of dialectical thinking. In this, Sartre is making a valuable contribution to Marxist philosophy.

In the *Critique* Sartre has broadened his concept of the dialectic; formerly he restricted its operation to the sphere of ideas (see Chapter Three, page 48). He now extends it to the human sphere in general: to man's interaction with the material world, with other individual men, and with groups of men. Explaining his conception of the dialectic, he states that it "is not a blind law but a *lived reality* resulting from the multitude of men acting within themselves and with one another dialectically."[12] He still refuses to grant the validity of the dialectic in the domain of matter or nature. In his present position Sartre maintains that the material world reacts dialectically only when man first acts upon it. Summarizing Sartre's views on these matters, Wilfrid Desan writes:

> If there is dialectic in nature, it can only be insofar as human praxis confers upon matter its particular "importance" or stated differently, insofar as material conditions affect the *human* world and in turn themselves receive the impact of human interference. Only within the social orbit of man can matter have dialectical implications. Outside man and without man, dialectic is mere hypothesis.[13]

This is an external dialectic and not internal to matter. Marxism, on the other hand, holds an internal dialectic of matter as well as an external dialectic of man's interaction with nature and with the material world.

Sartre's study, then, provides a detailed analysis of the role and the operation of the dialectic in man's interaction with the material and the social world. In the words of Desan, "*he wants to live with the reader all forms of life* and show their dialectical structures, then submit this to a 'critique.' His purpose is to show that there is place for a

Critical Dialectic to replace the *Dogmatic Dialectic* of certain Marxist theoreticians; . . ."[14]

The Material Dialectic

Proceeding with his study, Sartre finds that man acts upon the world, upon man, upon groups of men—and groups upon groups—and these, in turn, respond to his actions and react upon him. There is a circularity and a reciprocity in all activity. "The most important discovery of dialectical experience . . ." Sartre claims, "is that man is 'mediated' by things to the extent that things are mediated by man."[15] The originator of all activity therefore is man. He begins his activity because he is defined by a "lack" or a "need" and must act upon the surrounding world in order to overcome this "lack" or "need." In the course of his activity he *unifies* the plurality surrounding him and makes out of it a passive and inert totality which becomes an obstacle for him. This inert obstacle that man encounters applies both to nature and to other men. Sartre labels it the *antidialectic:* "The dialectic is free, controlled, planned; the antidialectic comes into play when the actions of man escape him and he becomes unfree, inert, passive. In the former he is master of his fate, in the latter, victim."[16]

Thus a good segment of the movements that man's activity constantly unleashes are beyond his control, and although he has a molding influence upon them they in turn have a molding influence upon him. He becomes unfree, inert, and passive in the sense that there is nothing he can do about the reciprocal activity of the material world and of other men which he himself originally unleashed through his "unifying" activity. Very often man is molded and influenced in a fashion that he was not able to foresee when he initiated his activity. It is in order to avoid these pitfalls of inertness and fatalism that man unites with others to form a *group*. For with the greater strength of the group it becomes possible to regain control of the dialectic.

The vehicle of all human activity is what Sartre calls *totalization*. Dialectical thought and practical activity are feasible only because of the individual's power of *totalization,* which is defined as a unifying activity that views parts as a connected whole while remembering that the whole thus observed is in process and never stationary or complete. The result or product of *totalization* is *totality* (also called a *practico-inert*)—or a picture. And the making or using of totalities is called *praxis*. Only the mind of the individual is capable of *totalization* or *praxis*.[17]

To illustrate these terms Sartre uses the example of an empty house as a *totality* (*practico-inert*); "but once inhabited, it becomes a home and the center of that unifying activity which is called 'totalization.' "[18] By placing a man in the window of the house, Sartre grants him the power to unify and "objectify" (make inert and passive) nature and other men. To use another of Sartre's illustrations, the man in the window may see two persons working in the fields. The persons are separated by a fence and unaware of each other's existence. But because of the man in the window who sees them at their separate activity, they become unified, categorized, and objectified. Sartre calls the man in the window "the third man." While observing the two men in the fields, this is what "the third man" thinks: "In the grasp of my own self, I understand their work and how their individual aims shape their labor and locates them in a class."[19] The man in the window is able to classify these men not because of some abstract principle in his mind but because of the material concreteness of the situation which he is observing. It is as if he were saying to himself: "There is no human nature, or universal character of man; there is only *this* farmer recognizable by his tools and his clothes or *this* construction worker, known through his praxis and his project."[20]

Illustrating further, Sartre describes a taxi driver passing the River Seine and observing a group of people, again strangers to each other, on the bank, watching something in the water. The taxi driver thus catches them in a common act, in a common intention: "In keeping this intention alive, the third man is mediator between a form of universality (the common deed and purpose of these men) and the different individuals themselves. *Unity is imposed upon them from the outside.*"[21]

Summarizing Sartre's theories up to this point, Wilfrid Desan writes:

> We have discovered that at the start there is an individual *praxis*. Upon leaving this "abstract" moment, we have seen the relations of men arise as an unavoidable dimension, each man with his own pro-ject and totalizing mental activity embracing the other. We have noticed also how these connections were cemented in and revealed through the inorganic materiality. Human beings are organisms, but these organisms live in a world of matter, use matter and constitute a plurality spread open over the inorganic. Their activities, each one of them, are caught up in diverse matter. This multiplicity and variety of material (and inorganic) conditions shape the relations of men and give them their individual and peculiar character.[22]

The methods of human thought, activity, and interaction are to be found in the dialectical processes described above. But the cause of all human activity is to be found in the psychological "lack" of man's consciousness and in the further material "lack" or "scarcity" that man finds in the world. It is this material scarcity that "is considered by Sartre to be the very foundation of human history, that which in our world has made it to be what it is."[23] It would appear that the mainsprings of man's activity are double—psychological "need" and material "scarcity." But that is a misleading notion, for we soon learn that there is scarcity in the material world only because man first put it there: "Scarcity reaches matter through man and man through matter."[24] The dialectical interaction is present, but it originates with the mind of man. However, as the argument develops this point of origin is de-emphasized by Sartre, and scarcity is defined more and more as a purely material phenomenon.

Proceeding further, we find that it is scarcity that gives rise to that important characteristic of every society—conflict. Scarcity is a threat to the individual's life and therefore produces an inhuman element in man, who says to himself: *"of a certain thing there is not enough, therefore I must negate you."*[25] And since all men are threatened by scarcity, interpersonal conflict is the result. In the *Critique*, however, Sartre is no longer interested in discussing this form of conflict in detail, and he quickly passes on to an examination of social conflict.

Because men, living in a certain area, are bounded by a specific physical space, they are confronted with common problems of overcoming material obstacles. Consequently these material obstacles *"totalize men into certain groups."*[26] Social conflict comes about if there is overlapping of boundaries or if a certain group is nomadic in habits or simply requires more room because of an increase in population or other needs. Group conflicts of this nature become wars. Thus, material scarcity, which man himself first posited on matter and on other men, becomes the cause of individual, group, and, later, class conflicts and wars.[27]

Now man attempts to overcome scarcity, but Sartre finds that regardless of where man turns he constantly becomes enslaved by the matter that he wishes to shape and control in order to satisfy his needs. Industrialization, with its unsavory features of class struggle, exploitation of labor, and the alienation of both laborers and employers from their product and from their true nature as men, is but a modern failure of man in his search for the elimination of scarcity. And even though man, both laborer and employer, enters into his work as a free being, as a free choice, in the end he finds himself enslaved by his own products. Paraphrasing Sartre on this point, Wilfrid Desan writes: "It is natural, therefore, that in the achievement of an *opus*, the creator both recognizes himself and finds there a stranger. For there is an Hegelian alienation at work: man discovers himself as *other* in the objectivity, and in objectivized matter, contemplates with sorrow the *antiman*."[28]

This final tragic result of every man's actions is true in man's work and relation with the material world as well as in his work and relation with society. In each case man begins as a free being, freely choosing a specific act, and in each case he ends as a slave alienated from the products of his actions. He cannot place the responsibility for the end results upon anything or anybody but himself, for in the end result he is able to recognize his own actions and desires. But Sartre is quick to emphasize that all this does not mean that freedom is lost, for in each case a new action and a new beginning may be made. Man is still free to accept or to reject the present as he finds it or as it has been formed by his or by other men's actions. Therefore Sartre argues that "the stringent limitations of freedom should not make us forget, however, that the *praxis* of men is free temporization, since it efficiently plans and reorganizes and shapes a future."[29]

The Social Dialectic

How man overcomes the limitations of his present freedom and reorganizes the future is best examined in man's action in the society. Thus after having reached a certain stage in his examination of man's relation with the material world, the natural dialectic of life itself leads Sartre to a study of man's relations with the social world.

Sartre finds, first and foremost, that society as a whole is characterized by its *series*, or by *sérialité*. The series is defined as "a juxtaposition of individuals, all of whom are defined within the collective ensemble as other, but have no further distinction."[30] And it is "characterized by its passive, inert, inorganic quality."[31] For example, an amalgamation of solitary individuals waiting for a bus forms a series. And Sartre stresses that this is a *real* and not an *ideal* entity. The entire society is composed of all types of series, and the individual, although he may not be aware of it, belongs to a good number of these series. Some of the series are transitory in character—the passengers waiting for a bus or riding in a bus—and others are more permanent—the bus driver, for instance. The entire panorama of series in a society constitutes the social environment in which the individual lives, acts, and is acted upon: "The seriality constitutes . . . a certain *milieu,* whether this be the cohesion of individuals, as Others, working within a certain profession, living within a certain section of a city, or belonging to a particular business collectivity, retail or wholesale."[32]

Notwithstanding its passivity and its lack of a clearly defined structure, the series is capable of exercising great power, as, for example, when the shopkeeper must take into consideration the *milieu* of customers and of other shopkeepers around him in determining his prices.

Since all men must live in these types of amorphous yet powerful and actual series, which subconsciously classify them and influence their actions, they are not free. Their life in society and in seriality determines their behavior and the behavior of others toward them. Sartre escapes this social determinism by arguing that even under these conditions man "is *not unfree.*" And he continues, that "on the contrary, one has to be man and free to be able to grasp the meanings of things and to execute the commands which they imply."[33] In addition, it is Sartre's contention that man considers every situation as provisional and as amenable to change.

In society, when a situation becomes unbearable for a number of individuals at the same time, the change is ef-

fected through the rise of the *group*. In more technical
language this is what occurs: "At a certain moment the
individual dialectic, on the basis of the materiality which
it cannot cross, will invent *new* media in a *new* social field
against the imperium of the practico-inert."[34] The new
media will be the group, and man's "eventual unification
through and in the group will be the negation of 'the impossibility of life which threatens the serial multiplicity.' "[35]
When speaking of the "practico-inert" and of the "serial
multiplicity," Sartre is referring to both the material and
the social aspects of seriality that begin to enslave, "negate," man. The relationship is always dialectical, and
one cannot speak of society without making reference
to the material conditions that "mediate" or shape and
classify the various elements of society.

Before a fully defined group is formed out of the inert
social seriality it must first pass through a process of birth.
In its fetal stage Sartre calls it the *groupe en fusion*. A
group does not arise organically from its own inner forces
or motives but must be triggered into existence by another
group. Such a development occurs when a particular series
is threatened in some manner by an already existing group.
The existing group's threat acts as a catalyst on the series
and coalesces its passive members into a unified group
bound together by a similarity of situation. Dialectical
reasoning enters at this point, and Sartre explains that
even though it is the outside group that gives birth to the
new group, it is the members of the new group that give
it life:

> There is a certain paradox in the fact that it is the
> outsider, the non-member who, in his viewing of the
> group, is necessary to constitute it, to give it its on-
> tological status, yet it is the insider, the member, who,
> through his act of totalization and mediated reci-
> procity, gives it its ontological character. Indeed, the
> practical and the ontological are in conflict.[36]

The group therefore has ontological being through the outsider, but it has practical being through the action of the *individual*. This is an important principle, and in order to elaborate upon it and also to demonstrate at some length the flavor of Sartre's dialectical thinking, a long quotation from Wilfrid Desan follows; it describes in detail an example of the genesis of one particular group:

Sartre, wishing to avoid oversimplification (and to demonstrate the freedom of the individual man, ever his preoccupation) reformulates the question in this way: What makes it possible for a member of a series, as for example, an inhabitant of the *quartier* Saint Antoine, to step into that structural unity which is called a group, and which as a group, can storm a Bastille? How does the impotent individual *decide by himself* to become power? To answer that question, we come back always to the common object, in our case the common danger—the Bastille as a power and a presence, the siege of the army—around which the seriality of the *quartier* Saint Antoine is orbiting. There are, furthermore, a certain number of relations which have paved the way for eventual unification, as, for example, the comradeships resulting from living in the same section, being involved in the same labor or belonging to the same class. Since there relations have up to now not excluded the impotency of the multitude *qua* multitude, something further must happen, nevertheless, in the strange phenomenon of group formation.

It is to the individual that we must turn at this stage of "*haute temperature historique.*" The organized totality (government, army) which threatens totalizes the non-group (the citizenry of Paris), drawing everyone from his being merely Other and making him the *third man* in relation to a certain constellation of reciprocities. This "third man" is freed of his

inert otherness, as object, and discovers a free inter-
individual reality as an *immediate* human relation;
the Other, passive object of the old series, freely becomes acting subject, who himself totalizes. It was a
hundred centers of syntheses which rallied together
to take the Bastille. For it is through this third man
that the practical unity is revealed and asserted as the
negation of an organized praxis—the onslaught of the
government, the army—which threatens them all.
"The third man, structurally speaking, is the human
mediation through which *directly* [from you to me,
me to you, man to man] the multiplicity of epicenters
and ends [individual centers of action, isolated from
one another in the seriality] makes itself organized as
determined by a synthetic objective." In other words,
when the outside group totalizes the multiplicity, the
latter totalizes itself; *the objective of the third man
becomes the common objective,* and it is felt as such
by him, he knows himself to be unified with all the
others by a common exigency. His danger is my danger, and vice versa. The inhabitant of the *quartier*
Saint Antoine is in grave peril, not as an isolated
bandit, whose eccentric behavior needs correction,
nor merely as *another* in the vague form of a seriality
like that of the market, but as an individual of that
section and of that particular political brand: *he is
wanted* and *he is object of a planned and totalizing
annihilation coming down upon all the Parisians of
the quartier.* It is "Versailles" which makes every inhabitant realize himself to be the third man.[37]

In the stage described above the group is still *en
fusion,* for it is motivated primarily by the spontaneous
activity and totalization of distinct but united individuals
—all of them now in the role of the *third man*—that form
it and synthesize it. And since it is each individual who
through his free choice synthesizes the plurality into a

united group, every individual member of that group is also free. All the individuals make the same choice, and no one is imposed upon. Whatever controls and limitations there may be in the *groupe en fusion,* they are the controls and limitations that each individual imposes upon himself for the sake of a greater freedom.

The *groupe en fusion,* however, is in movement and cannot remain in its original state for an extended period of time. The force of circumstances lead either to its dissolution and return to *sérialité,* or to its crystallization into a stable and clearly defined *group.* Thus when the *groupe en fusion* in the example above achieves its objective and captures the Bastille it must either organize into a disciplined group with leaders and rules or face the threat of dissolution and chaos. If the group is to maintain order and discipline it will, in time, be compelled to rely upon threats against its own members. Sartre states that the group's internal discipline is achieved first by the *oath* (either explicit or implicit) that all the members of the group make uniting them in a common purpose, and second, by *Terreur,* or threat, since the oath without penalties attached to it would be empty. Once the *groupe en fusion* has reached this level of development it becomes an actual *group* and begins its further evolution toward an institution, and later toward that most institutionalized form of a group—the bureaucracy.

Describing these new elements in Sartre's thoughts, Desan writes:

> In truth, the *terreur* is actually a natural development of a group, any group. It is not a minority dictating its will through violence, but it is myself and all of us involved in a mutual distrust and a mutual hope, the hope of consolidating the group through consolidating the inert within us. The oath provides one basis of the inert, but this basis is insufficient. The *terreur* is an attempt (however vain) to produce in the group

an ontological unity instead of a mere practical unity. Everyone now becomes an inorganic thing through which the purpose will be accomplished, and the freedom which is left is the freedom of the group not of the individual, except as he finds it through the group. When individual freedom is alienated, or entrusted to the group, and only the "function" is left, we are on our way to what we call an institution. This implies two main transformations: the introduction of a certain desired inertia, and the appearance of authority.[38]

Therefore, as soon as a stable organization is achieved and the group develops into an institution the individual, and his freedom, becomes submerged in the organization and is useful only as an obedient functionary. As a matter of fact, in an institution the individual who insists upon his individuality and upon his free initiative may become dangerous:

> As an immediate result, the institution has a greater stability and a greater rigidity, but it has also by the same token a strong power of *inertia*, since it considers the ultimate purpose and the immediate function as *essential* and the individual as *unessential*. In this situation, any individual who proposes a change is suspect, for that is by itself a revelation of his individual freedom. A *group* becomes *institution* when there is an impotency towards alteration. It remains directed upon a common objective, but it is frozen through the internal alternity, which is, as we know, characteristic of seriality. Yet it works.[39]

And so the dialectical circle has once again run its full course. Whichever way man turns, whether to matter or to society, he still ends by losing his freedom; and always it is he himself who is responsible for initiating the activity that later engulfs him and deprives him of his individuality and his freedom. He alone remains responsible, and there is no one to blame for the hopeless outcome but himself and the fates who made him as he is and the world as it is.

It was the individual who first posited scarcity in the material world. Then when he made attempts to conquer this scarcity he became embroiled in physical and institutional processes that caused his alienation from the products of his activities and so enslaved him. When he turned to society seeking aid in overcoming material threats to his well-being and survival, he gave birth to a group which again later developed into a rigid institution that was no longer responsive to his individual wishes. On the contrary, the institution deprived him of his freedom and made him into its functionary. Once more he became alienated from the social manifestations that his own activities unleashed, and was enslaved by them.

It is not necessary to follow Sartre's further detailed development of the dialectic's operation in society; the development describes the evolution of the group into a progressively more rigid institution and its bureaucracy, and then proceeds to provide definitions of the state and of the sovereign based upon the former concepts. The main principles of Sartre's philosophical position, however, have been examined, and what remains is but a natural development and illustration of that position.

It is, nevertheless, imperative to add that once the group reaches a certain stage in its growth it must of necessity evolve along the lines chartered by Sartre: from the loose group to the inflexible bureaucracy, from the importance of the individual to the importance of his function, from freedom to the loss of freedom. Once more Sartre maintains that the individual is *not unfree*, that at each point in this evolutionary process he may step out of it and regain his original freedom. But when faced with the dialectical reality of matter and society, both of which can act only to alienate and to enslave him in an endless repetitive cycle, there is little that can be said of such a deceptive freedom. It is freedom to escape in order to be caught again.

Sartre is fully cognizant of the severe limitations of this "freedom to escape" and in the end must consent to the harsher but more realistic definition of freedom as the "awareness of necessity." For it is the only definition of freedom that is consistent with his semi-deterministic theories. Wilfrid Desan formulates this in the following manner: "The dialectic which moves through history is not merely deterministic; at every stage—individual, serial, group—the free individual intervenes. If he cannot control, he can at least be *aware* of the events which are operating."[40] Or again, "It is impossible to underestimate the importance of a clear insight, or what we have been calling 'comprehension,' for the loss of comprehension is the loss of freedom itself."[41] And Desan informs the reader that comprehension and awareness of the operations of history are the purpose of Sartre's book. (The same contention, interestingly enough, was made concerning the writings of Marx.)

In concluding his book, Sartre ends not with a note on the need for freedom and on how the individual may safeguard his freedom—the topic which supposedly was his aim and his preoccupation—but with a note on the inevitability of determinism:

> Sartre concludes with a summary that emphasizes once more the increasing institutionalization of the group as an inevitable phenomenon. The same air of fatalism which we have observed earlier hangs heavily over this passage, with only the previous plea for "the critical experience" to lift the oppressive weight of inertia. Thus the unity of the group is seen to lie in its object, in the groups exterior to it, in each of its members as excluded third, ultimately, in the activity of the sovereign, to whom power is delegated. The

power is never really *in* the group itself, except through the powerlessness of its members, a powerlessness which gives the material functions a greater power and inertia. The true efficiency of the group lies in its immersion in the matter, but where this happens completely, where *praxis* becomes *processus* and action becomes inert and passive, the common ends are no longer controllable. Without ceasing to be the common ends of the group, they become destinies.[42]

In other words, even the group which was originally formed as a means of overcoming the threats of the material practico-inert and of the passive social seriality has itself become entombed in matter and passivity. It has lost its ability to control and to act upon its aims, and become a helpless pawn in the dialectical movement of the world.

The Union Fails

Critique de la Raison Dialectique, like *Being and Nothingness,* is an imposing philosophical creation; if anything, it contains more pronounced elements of maturity, self-sufficiency, and harmony than the earlier work. And it proves once again that true philosophy is an art, and that a great philosopher is a creative person, an artist, and not only an intellectual involved with dull analysis—induction and deduction. Like the artist, the philosopher describes life and the world and unveils new vistas of thought and experience through his own insight and vision. Only a matter of technique separates the artist from the philosopher.

In his latest philosophical endeavor Sartre has created an entirely new vocabulary for the purpose of describing material and social phenomena that have never been dealt with before in similar connotations. He has indicated new paths in our understanding of man's interrelationship and interdependence with the material world. He has provided new psycho-sociological insights into that broad, inert, and passive element of society which he has defined as a series; he has indicated how this series lives and acts in relation to the individual who is part of it; he has shown how this unconscious and inactive series becomes transformed into a conscious and purposeful group; he has further shown how this group inevitably evolves into an institution and later into a bureaucracy, both of which act to stifle individual freedom and individual initiative; and he has brilliantly treated the old but basic elements of every society—scarcity, conflict, violence, classes, the state, and the sovereign. Throughout his study he has continuously directed his focus upon the individual, examining the effects of all the above movements and elements upon the individual's thought and behavior and particularly upon his freedom. For it is a fact that Sartre set upon this venture with the purpose of bridging the gap between the Marxist conception of a determined society and history and the Existentialist conception of the free and creative individual.

Before stating any conclusions about the results of this ambitious theoretical adventure, it is now possible and necessary to broach a number of observations criticizing the basic theories expounded in the *Critique*. It should be borne in mind, however, that these are but preliminary criticisms, and a more thorough analysis is called for in order fully to support and substantiate such observations. A detailed analysis, unfortunately, is outside the scope of this book; our main interest at this juncture lies in describing Sartre's success or failure in forging a philosophical union between Marxism and Existentialism.

As a first critical observation, it would appear that the most fundamental concept of *Critique de la Raison Dialectique, totalization* with its various ramifications and appendages, is actually the usual concept of *dialectical reasoning*. Sartre's contribution to this concept is its segmentation into a number of distinct parts, thereby providing a more precise definition of the dialectic, and also the incorporation of human psychology as a necessary part of dialectical reasoning if the latter is to serve as a true method for understanding man and his activity in the world. The definitions of *totalization, totality, practico-inert,* and *praxis* are all important concepts that aid in providing a more precise comprehension of dialectical reasoning and its operation. (The Marxist objection that Sartre places the entire responsibility for the function of the dialectic on the mind of the individual will be treated later.)

There is, in addition, a definite, new insight into the functioning of the dialectic, or, what is more to the point, into the activity of man, with Sartre's description of the limitations on man's ability to control the results of his actions and the results of the reactions of other men and of the material world. In his exposition of these phenomena, Sartre implicitly relies upon his former concept of the *en-soi,* of the entire world's constant escape into the "facticity" of inert matter which has its own laws of existence and is independent of and separate from the influence of man. In the *Critique,* Sartre labels this process the *antidialectic.* The major difference between the *en-soi* and the *antidialectic* is that the *en-soi* had no involuntary influence on man, whereas the *antidialectic* has a very definite involuntary one. Between the *en-soi* (the material world) and the *pour-soi* (man's consciousness) there could be no union, even though the *pour-soi* yearned for such a union. But now, between the *antidialectic* and man's consciousness, a union is not only possible, but becomes imperative. The individual initiates activities which soon reverberate and influence his further activities. It is exactly here that Sartre abandons the Existentialist notion of absolute individual freedom and proposes a degree of fatalism. His conclusive reasoning on this point is difficult to grasp, for now, like the Marxists, he requires both an element of determinism and an element of freedom to be able to substantiate a social theory that would permit of purposeful human activity.

This new determinism of Sartre's is more vivid in his representations of the evolution of society from the principle of material scarcity to the resulting struggles and conflicts among men and to the development of groups, institutions, bureaucracies, and states. Aside from the consent of the individual needed in the formation of the *groupe en fusion* (which, by the way, came into being only because of the activity of another group), there is no human volition or direction involved in this evolutionary process. And when history is defined as the constant movement of groups arising out of seriality, evolving into complex institutions and then retiring into inert seriality, then truly there remains very little for the individual to do.[43] The individual is indispensable at the beginning, when his mind serves to *totalize* the group, but once this is completed the individual, *qua* individual, is unnecessary to the group, as well as a threat if he insists upon retaining his individuality and his freedom. But upon reflection it becomes apparent that even the initial activity of the individual in totalizing the group is the outcome of causes operating outside of the individual and over which he has little control. And Sartre maintains that such a determined evolutionary process is a true and factual picture of social life.

This clearly indicates how far Sartre has moved away from the totally sovereign individual who stood alone and above society and history. The only remnant of that Existentialist individual is Sartre's claim that at each moment of this evolution the individual is still free to escape and stand outside of it. But that would only place him back in the inert and passive seriality; and Sartre does not have much respect for that element of society.

With the possibility of escape comes the matter of responsibility. If the individual is free at each moment to renounce the results of his and of the world's actions, then he is also responsible for all his actions and for the results of these actions. If he does not wish to break away from the processes of social evolution and from the *antidialectical* activity of the material world, he still remains responsible, for this choice is also a free choice. But a total responsibility of this type is in contradiction to the thesis that man is not in full control of all the results of his actions and of all the events in which he must participate. The *antidialectical* nature of reality—both material and social —often leads him to actions that he would not otherwise freely undertake. If his control is not total, then his responsibility cannot be total—except in some higher metaphysical sense. Such a metaphysic was acceptable and consistent with Sartre's ideas in *Being and Nothingness*, but it is no longer warranted in the *Critique* where he deals with reality from a more materialistic point of view.

Individual freedom and individual responsibility are two basic principles that Sartre hoped to incorporate into Marxism. It is evident from the foregoing paragraphs into what neglect these two principles have fallen and to what extent their power has been diminished by Sartre's own argumentation. The freedom that Sartre has salvaged for the individual is truly an empty one. He is giving him the choice between god and beast. What does it mean in practice to refuse to go along with the evolution and the dialectic of material and social phenomena? At each moment of the evolution man may disengage himself—but where does that place him? What can he do in his new position? What will the attitude and the behavior of society be toward a man who constantly initiates actions and organizations only to forsake them as soon as they become operative and productive? And yet, if the individual desires to remain true to his free nature and not become alienated, this is exactly what he must do. He will therefore become a restless rebel or revolutionary or perhaps be classified as neurotic and insane by a society which judges its members by the standards of the majority. The speculations about this questionable freedom of the individual to "break away" can proceed along similar critical lines, and in no foreseeable case are the results happy or realistic.

Faced with such a fruitless situation and already in the midst of deterministic thinking, it is a logical step for Sartre to proceed to the sober redefinition of freedom as the *awareness of reality,* or, in other words, the recognition of necessity. This Hegelian and Marxian definition of freedom, it must be noted, is in logical conflict with the definition of freedom as the right of man to "break away." The awareness of reality means that once a man realizes and recognizes the necessary operation of the dialectic in the material and in the social spheres, he will not make foolish and hopeless attempts to escape the dialectical laws of the world. True freedom cannot consist in blind rebellion against the normal functioning of the universe. True freedom must consist of an understanding of the principles that govern the world, its matter and society, and in the ability that such an understanding provides for at least modifying the practical results of the less desirable principles. This Marxist corollary to the definition of freedom as the recognition of necessity is valid. Now that Sartre has accepted the definition, he must also accept the logical corollary. The freedom to "break away" is only a metaphysical deception that can have no realistic function in the practical world.

In the course of his arguments, Sartre mentions a third conception of freedom: that man is free because he must be able to "grasp the meaning of things and to execute the commands which they imply."[44] This notion of freedom is consistent with the definition of freedom as the awareness of reality. But upon analysis it turns out that it only means that man is free to make himself a slave. Indeed, the sentence following the quotation given above clearly points to that direction: "Even the worker freely engages himself, although he knows that the machine will be his prison and his alienation."[45]

Thus, despite Sartre's sincere claims to the contrary, he has entrapped himself in the Marxist net on the question of freedom, and is now vulnerable to the usual critiques of Marxism on the points of determinism and freedom.

Aside from the more dominant issues of the dialectic, of freedom, determinism, and responsibility, there are a number of less vital but still interesting aspects of Sartre's *Critique*, to which we now briefly turn.

One of the major obstacles to the feasibility of a social theory in *Being and Nothingness* was the sharp division between the *pour-soi* and the *en-soi*. Apparently in the *Critique* this sharp cleavage is overcome. Wilfrid Desan, however, in commenting on Sartre's new position, thinks that the cleavage remains:

> Sartre's Subject attempts in vain to dominate the group, just as in *L'Etre et le Neant*, his *Pour-soi* was a vain effort to conquer the Other. The appropriation of other men and of the world was doomed to failure, just as is the domination of the group through the Subject, for the obvious reason that neither individual man nor *Pour-soi* are made for domination of what is above and beyond.[46]

It is true that in *Being and Nothingness* the failure of a union between the *pour-soi* and the *en-soi* was due to the impossibility on the part of the *pour-soi* to conquer and control the *en-soi*. Sartre admitted the failure. The cleavage was also characterized by the absence of any interaction or interrelationship between the *pour-soi* and the *en-soi*, and the perpetual escaping of the *en-soi* from the *pour-soi's* field of activity.

In the *Critique*, it is still true that the individual is not able to conquer and control the material and the social worlds. Here Desan's point is valid. But now the need to conquer and control is of a totally different nature than it was in *Being and Nothingness*, and there is also a very definite dialectical interaction and interrelationship be-

tween the individual's consciousness and the outside
world. In the *Critique* the outside world escapes only *partially* into the inert materiality or "facticity" and, instead
of remaining inert, reacts upon man's consciousness and
influences his further activity. In this sense there is a material and real bridge between man's consciousness and
the outside world which was absent between the *pour-soi*
and the *en-soi*. In Sartre's present work there is a dialectical interaction between the organic and the conscious and
the inorganic and the unconscious.

The famous Existentialist distinction between authentic
and unauthentic existence has undergone severe alterations in the *Critique*. In *Being and Nothingness* the type
of existence—authentic or unauthentic—that the individual
led depended entirely upon his will and his consciousness.
In the *Critique*, although it is still true that the individual
must retain consciousness of his freedom in order to live
authentically, the choice of a free and therefore authentic
existence is not always practical or even *his* to make. We
have described above what the consequences are for an
individual who insists upon retaining his individual freedom at all costs. Sartre does not deal with the authentic-
unauthentic distinction in the *Critique*, and it may be assumed that it is no longer operative in the new world that
he has described there. But he does deal with the related
matter of alienation; and here again it develops that the
individual has little or no control over the phenomenon,
for as soon as he begins to think and to act, alienation
comes as an inevitable process, in the forms of the *antidialectic* and the *antiman*, and quickly precipitates around
his life so that he becomes alienated in the classical Marxist fashion. Previously alienation resided in the mind of
the individual and could be overcome by a change of
consciousness. Now alienation is the result of the individual's interaction with the world and can be overcome only
through new activity. This is an obvious turn away from

the Existentialist and closer to the Marxist position on the matter of alienation.

Another obstacle to a social theory in *Being and Nothingness* was the definition of conflict. Conflict was the result of the ontological structure of human consciousness with its need to posit everything and everyone but itself as an *en-soi*, a thing. This ontological procedure gave rise to unavoidable interpersonal conflict, because every man —who knows himself to be a *pour-soi*, a subject—objects to being made into an *en-soi*, an inert, passive object. In the *Critique* this form of ontological conflict is not mentioned; instead, conflict is now caused by the material fact of scarcity. But the end consequences are even worse than before; where previously the conflict was on a metaphysical plane, it now descends to the physical level, and actual violence and death follow.

Sartre argues that scarcity is a real threat to man's survival. The presence of other men in the face of scarcity is an extension of that threat. Every man, therefore, views every other man as a material obstacle that must be overcome, subjugated, or controlled if he is to survive. This is the cause of violence and war. Thus we have returned again by another path to the eternal conflict among men, and the less philosophical and more political martial strains of the Hobbesian "war of all against all" again resound in the air. And since scarcity is not material but psychological in point of origin, even if men achieve a world of abundance the notion of scarcity will remain, and with it conflict.

A question also arises as to the universality of human nature in reference to the matter of scarcity. Must all men react in the same manner to the material world so that they endow it with scarcity? And even if they find scarcity in the material world, must they, of necessity, view other men as threats to their survival? Is not the matter of scarcity, regardless of whether it is material or psychological in origin or in fact, a relative phenomenon to which every individual reacts differently? Are not a charitable attitude and behavior possible instead of an attitude of selfishness and fear?

Scarcity serves to unite men into groups. This is possible only if all men respond to scarcity in the same manner. *Totalization* is the means through which men unite into groups. But this, too, is possible only if all men *totalize* in an identical manner. Sartre's assumption appears to be that all men do react to scarcity and do *totalize* in exactly the same manner when confronted by exactly the same situation. But this means that Sartre has lost the subjective individual and replaced him by a predictable automaton. And this again is in keeping with a deterministic theory of society and of the world.

It may be objected that the loss of individual subjectivity is only temporary, and that it is not a loss of subjectivity in fact, because every individual has freely made the same decision. Nonetheless, temporary or not, it is lost, and its loss leads to a more permanent and institutionalized loss of individual subjectivity and freedom. As for the free decision, it is the free decision to grasp and comprehend the laws of the world, which we have shown is the deterministic view of freedom, that permits the individual to freely enslave himself; if he does not do it freely, it will be done for him by the dialectical principles that govern the world.

Actually, Sartre makes an implied admission of the subjectivity of the individual in the argument that a group cannot remain united for long unless it begins to rely upon the oath and *Terreur*. The oath and *Terreur* are required in order to control the recalcitrant individuals who wish to follow their own subjective ends instead of the common ends of the group. The group consequently denies the individual his subjectivity of purpose and fixes the common purpose as the only acceptable one; it "objectifies" or makes inert that purpose and with it the individuals who must now serve that purpose under the threat of force.

An inconsistency in reasoning may be observed here.

All men, we first learned, react similarly to scarcity, and all men *totalize* similarly to form a group when confronted by a common threat. The reaction is universal and predictable. This element of universality and predictability is characteristic of the series as well. But once in the group, men may pursue subjective and unpredictable goals, so that *Terreur* is needed to make their actions more predictable and certain. The problem in reasoning here lies in the old attempt to combine determinism and freedom, in this case, objectivity and subjectivity. Both are necessary in a theory that wishes to hold a degree of universal determinism and a degree of subjective freedom. The two elements do not mix readily, and there is always the question of distinguishing where one begins and the other ends. Thus, once more, Sartre demonstrates his present affinity for concepts characteristic of Marxism.

Lastly, in one of his comments on Sartre's new theories, Wilfrid Desan notes that there is a current of hidden Manicheism running underneath these theories.[47] Sartre does indeed seem to echo Hobbes' belief that man at heart is evil and constantly in conflict with his fellow men over the matter of self-survival. Sartre does not discuss ethics in the *Critique,* most probably because ethics have little meaning and function in a determined world. But if he were to construct an ethical system it would have to reflect the influence of that Manicheism and would have to maintain that everything that is an obstacle to self-survival is evil and everything that aids self-survival is justified and good. There is little difference between this ethic and the Marxist-Leninist one which states that all that aids the proletariat in its struggle for supremacy is morally justified and good.

I mentioned earlier in this chapter that in *Critique de la Raison Dialectique* Sartre has forsaken Existentialism and has become a Marxist of a Sartrean mold. The Sartrean influence must be emphasized, for there are still cer-

tain very basic differences between his theories and the
theories of orthodox Marxism. For example, Marxists will
not readily admit the psychological and sociological additions that Sartre wishes to incorporate into the dialectical
comprehension and description of matter, history, society,
and the individual. And it is exactly these two sciences
that Sartre has relied upon heavily in his theorizing about
dialectical phenomena. But mainly Marxists would object
to the continued glorification of the subjective, autono-
mous individual who, according to Sartre, is responsible
for the origin of the dialectical process in thought, in matter, in action, in society, and in history. It is the individual
who posits scarcity in the material world, and it is the
individual who through his power of *totalization* creates
the groups, which in turn develop into the institutions that
direct and lead the movements of society. True, the individual is "mediated" and influenced by the processes
and the institutions that he sets in motion; this is the power
of the natural dialectic over which he has no control. But
it is he himself who initiates the activity of the dialectic,
and it is he who remains responsible for it. In the last
analysis, it is the individual who is responsible for all the
movements of society and history.

This emphasis upon the power of the individual in origi-
nating the processes of activity and history is really all
that remains of Sartre's basic Existentialist views. And
even this individual, as we have seen, bears little resem-
blance to the subjective and totally free individual of *Being and Nothingness*. Still, Marxists cannot consent even to
such a greatly qualified version of the individual, for they
maintain that the dialectic is present in the world without
the intervention and aid of the individual, that its laws of
operation, in the material world particularly, are independent of the individual, and that in the social world it is a
dialectical law by which society molds and directs the individual and not vice versa. Sartre's views on the dialectic

and on the individual would still be labeled as *bourgeois idealism.*

Although there is but one major concept—greatly altered—that has remained from the Existentialism of *Being and Nothingness,* there are many concepts in the *Critique* that reflect the dominant theories of Marxism. And it has been shown that even the one remaining Existentialist concept, the sovereign individual, has been brought closer to a Marxist (deterministic) character. Other notions that are new for Sartre but which carry a Marxist stamp include: the dialectical description of nature and society; the element of determinism and involuntarism in man's relationship with the material and social spheres; the determined or fatalistic evolution of certain social phenomena; the loss of the individual, his freedom, and subjectivity in the inevitable processes of social development; the description of material scarcity as a basis for social conflict and class warfare. In addition, we must mention the *de facto* loss or diminution of moral responsibility, both group and individual, in the presence of powerful elements of determinism.

The above enumeration indicates an acceptance on Sartre's part of a good number of the main deterministic and dialectical aspects of Marxism. Yet he will most certainly be criticized by Marxists for his silence on the other major theories of Marxism. He has ignored the role of economics or of the factors of production and their dialectical operation in society and history almost completely. He has failed to underscore the classical Marxist formulations of class struggle, of the proletarian revolution, and of the inevitability of the future classless society. Perhaps Sartre has taken the theory of socialism and these Marxist corollaries for granted and thinks that they are minor details that in no way clash with his more general theories. But that is still a moot question. The classless society, for instance, would face great difficulties finding a place for itself in the midst of Sartre's theories concerning the origin of scarcity, the *totalization* of groups, and their inevitable development into institutions and bureaucracies. On the other hand, the dictatorship of the proletariat could fit in harmoniously with these and other theories of the *Critique*. Or perhaps Sartre ignored these matters as too detailed to warrant attention in the face of the more fundamental merging of Marxism and Existentialism: the details could be attended to later.

Yet even with the merging of the fundamental concepts of the two philosophies, Sartre's success is very much in doubt. As we have demonstrated, instead of adding a helpful dose of free and creative Existentialism to deterministic and stultifying Marxism, Sartre has managed to do the opposite: he has buried Existentialism in a Marxism of his own making, and in the process he has lost precisely those concepts that he believed Marxism required if it were to serve as a true and complete philosophy for modern times—the free, subjective, creative, and purposeful individual; moral responsibility; and personal humanism.

Thus the attempted union of Marxism and Existentialism has failed. *Critique de la Raison Dialectique* is an illegitimate child that neither the Marxists nor the Existentialists will acknowledge as their own. If it has any influence and success in the coming future, it will be as a distinct and separate philosophy, although one that resembles Marxism more closely than Existentialism. It could be defined as Sartrean Marxism; and perhaps to the long list of Marxist revisionists we may now add the name of Jean-Paul Sartre.

Conclusion

The examination of Marxism and Existentialism, their arguments with each other and their relation to each other is now completed. We have found two philosophies with the same place of birth—in Hegel; with the same conceptions of human nature and consciousness—as vacuums whose essence is created in activity; with similar beliefs concerning ethics and history—as relative and open, man being the creator of values and history. But in all these apparently fundamental identities we have also found great disagreements once the respective philosophies began to develop their theories in detail. From the beginning to the end, the basic difference is a radically opposed conception of the individual. On this concept no reconciliation is possible; if it were, atheistic Existentialism would truly lose its *raison d'être* and Sartre's dream of a union would become a reality. For, as we have seen, even with a greatly diffused concept of the individual in *Critique de la Raison Dialectique* this concept is still the major obstacle to the harmonious merger of Marxism and Existentialism. A reconciliation, even if theoretically possible, would probably be harmful, for with all its faults, contemporary Existentialism, whether atheistic or religious, does provide one of the most vibrant and living antidotes to the Marxist view of the individual as an insignificant part of a materialistically determined world.

If there is a lesson to be derived from the study and examination of the confrontation between Marxism and Existentialism it is that man is *both* an individual and a social being. By seeing only the individual Existentialism lost society, and by seeing only society Marxism lost the individual. These are the extremes of a truth that lies somewhere in the middle. The philosophies with their distinct emphases of study do contribute indispensably to our knowledge of the individual and of society. An examination of them therefore reveals truths not to be found in any other manner, but it also underscores the elementary fact that a true theory of the individual and society is possible only with a thorough psychological and sociological knowledge of these two interrelated—individual and social —aspects of human existence. Because in all cases we deal here with fluid matter, with a process, with both subjectivity and objectivity, a true theory will not be one that is stable and absolute; a true theory will be one that takes

into account the process and the subjective-objective existence of humanity. Sartre was correct in sensing the need
of such a union, which he attempted in the *Critique*. Unfortunately, he went from one extreme to the other by
swinging too far to the left, and, like Marxism, losing the
free and creative individual in a determined world. Sartre's
failure may be attributed to the nature of the two philosophies he attempted to join. His failure does not mean
that a union of the individual and the social, of the subjective and the objective, is not feasible. It indicates only
that the instruments and the "compounds" used in his case
were not the correct ones. He might have been more successful if he had formulated a totally new social theory
with no reference to and no influence from Marxism. But
that would be asking too much of a man who has made
definite commitments to that philosophy, particularly in its
social aspects.

Again, because every theory depends upon the understanding of what man is, what society is, what should be
the relationship between them, and what the reason and
the purpose of each of these is, no theory can claim in-
fallibility unless it is able to provide absolute answers to
these fundamental questions of existence. Perhaps both
Existentialism and Marxism are in error on these questions,
and their further development of theories based upon the
erroneous basis only compounds the error.

The situation is fluid in more ways than one; the answers to the above questions vary with different philosophies, which often are able to change man to suit their
descriptions, at least to a significant degree. This much,
however, is clear: if man has no basic nature at all and
can be changed in any way, to any purpose, then no real
theory of the individual and of society is necessary, for the
theory is simply the recognition of the reality that happens
to exist at a particular time and in a particular place. But
if man does have a nature that characterizes him, a nature
that is both independent and dependent, then a theory is

possible and necessary. Such a theory would come closest to the truth and would be humanistic as well, if it correctly understood and interpreted the real nature and purpose of man and society. Then the theory could describe how best to attain a harmonious interaction between them and a useful development of man's life as both an individual and a social being.

The tragedy of man's life is that he walks in darkness. Through the bitter experience of trial and error he has learned to put up certain guideposts along his path, but his surroundings, his destination, and his purpose remain mysteries. Under such conditions he has made attempts to understand himself, the society, and the world he inhabits, and on the basis of his limited understanding builds elaborate theories, all of which have been defaced or buried by the sands of time.

NOTES

Chapter One

1. Marxist materialism should not be confused with "pure" or "vulgar" materialism; some of its most basic principles, such as the dialectical development of matter and history, and the transformation of quantity to quality, bespeak of a philosophy which openly rejects a purely mechanical interpretation of the universe. Indeed, Engels in "Ludwig Feuerbach" inveighs against the eighteenth-century materialism as mechanical and unhistorical—unaware of Darwin and Hegel. More recently, the great philosophic debates of the 1920s in the Soviet Union also culminated in the exorcism of mechanist and machinist interpretations of Marxist materialism.

2. Friedrich Engels, "Ludwig Feuerbach and the End of Classical German Philosophy," in *Basic Writings on Politics and Philosophy: Karl Marx and Friedrich Engels*, Lewis S. Feuer, ed. (New York: 1959), p. 210.

3. The first "turning back" of the mind on its parent—matter—may be considered a definition of elementary consciousness, a consciousness which is aware of matter and can experience it, but as yet cannot understand it; this is the consciousness common to animals. Man's consciousness differs in that it "turns back" on the fact that it is "turning back"; it is conscious of its consciousness: this is a definition of the ego. And

it is also only at this stage of consciousness that an understanding of matter and of its processes arises. The transformation of matter to both of these forms of consciousness are accounted for by the law of transformation of quantity (organic matter) to quality (consciousness).

In connection with this idea Lenin says: "Materialism, in full agreement with natural science, takes matter as primary and regards consciousness, thought and sensation as secondary, because in its well-defined form sensation is associated only with the higher forms of matter (organic matter), while 'in the foundation of the structure of matter' one can only surmise the existence of a faculty akin to sensation." V. I. Lenin, *Materialism and Empirio-Criticism: Critical Comments on a Reactionary Philosophy* (Moscow: 1947), p. 38.

4. A. G. Spirkin, "On the Nature of Consciousness," *Voprosy Filosofii*, XV, No. 6 (June 1961), p. 126. Unless otherwise indicated, all translations from Russian works are original.

Classical Marxism only indicates the broad outlines of the matter of consciousness, with its concomitants —perception, thought, and language. This essay, therefore, utilizes the later developments in this area of recent or contemporary orthodox Marxists.

5. Ibid., p. 118.

6. Lenin, op. cit., p. 44.

7. Spirkin, op. cit., p. 122.

8. Lenin, op. cit., p. 191.

9. Karl Marx, *A Contribution to the Critique of Political Economy* (Chicago: 1911), Author's Preface, pp. 11–12.

10. Engels, *Herr Eugen Dühring's Revolution in Science* (New York: 1934), p. 130.

11. Marx, "Theses on Feuerbach," Marx and Engels *Basic Writings*, op. cit., p. 244.

12. Engels, "Engels to Joseph Bloch," ibid., p. 398.

13. Ibid.

14. Marx and Engels, *Manifesto of the Communist Party* (New York: 1948), p. 19.

15. Marx, *A Contribution to the Critique of Political Economy,* loc. cit.

16. Jean-Paul Sartre, "Existentialism is a Humanism," *Existentialism from Dostoevsky to Sartre,* Walter Kaufmann, ed. (New York: 1956), pp. 290–91. It must be pointed out that this existential argument is not one of logical relations; even though one may grant that existence precedes essence, that is, that man exists before he becomes conscious of his existence and of himself as a man, it does not follow that because of this man makes his own essence. The essence could be given also, and man may only discover it as he discovers his existence.

17. From what may be called a purely technical point, yet still important, Sartre's Existentialism requires an underpinning on which to place the *cogito;* it finds such a base in the "pre-reflexive *cogito.*" This is simply consciousness without self-consciousness; the true *cogito* is the reflexive human consciousness: I know that I know.

18. Sartre, "Existentialism Is a Humanism," op. cit., p. 302.

19. Forrest Williams and Robert Kirkpatrick, Translators' Introduction to *The Transcendence of the Ego: An Existentialist Theory of Consciousness* (New York: 1962), pp. 21–22.

20. Ibid., p. 21.

21. Ibid., p. 22.

22. Maurice Natanson, *A Critique of Jean-Paul Sartre's Ontology* (University of Nebraska: 1951), p. 50.

23. Sartre, "Existentialism Is a Humanism," op. cit., p. 300.

24. Natanson, op. cit., p. 24.

25. Sartre, "Existentialism Is a Humanism," p. 295.

26. Ibid., p. 303.

27. Natanson, op. cit., p. 48.

28. Sartre, "Existentialism Is a Humanism," p. 294.

29. Sartre, from "Being and Nothingness" in *Existentialism and Human Emotions* (New York: 1957), p. 57.

30. Ibid., p. 59.

31. Sartre, "Existentialism Is a Humanism," p. 303.

Chapter Two

1. Jean-Paul Sartre, "Materialism and Revolution," *Literary and Philosophical Essays* (New York: 1962), p. 200.

2. Ibid., p. 201. Sartre traces the materialist dislike for metaphysics to the positivists, but he claims that the positivists were more logical, for they took no stand on the existence of God, considering all speculation on that subject unverifiable; they did the same with the question of the relation between the body and the mind. See p. 200 of the work cited here.

3. Friedrich Engels, *Ludwig Feuerbach and the Outcome of Classical German Philosophy* (New York: 1934), pp. 30–31.

4. Sartre, "Materialism and Revolution," p. 202.

5. Ibid.

6. Ibid., p. 203.

7. Ibid.

8. Ibid. The criteria cited by Sartre are also Hume's criteria, who, even by Engels' admission in *Ludwig Feuerbach,* is not an idealist but an agnostic.

9. Ludwig Feuerbach, the nineteenth-century German philosopher who by Engels' own admission forms the intermediate link between Hegel and Marx. It was Feuerbach who definitely broke with Hegelian idealism by arguing that nothing exists outside of nature and man and that religious ideas are but fantastic reflections of man's own essence. Feuerbach, however,

substituted his own religious reflections concerning the true socialism that could be constructed upon "love" among all men. Marx, of course, rejected this religious reflection and substituted his own scientific one. Also, because Feuerbach denied Hegel's doctrine of the *Weltgeist,* he stressed the role of the individual in determining his own history, consciousness, and thought. Marx, on the other hand, preferred to assign this role to society as a whole. In the emphasis on the individual's determining role in life and history, Feuerbach is also the intermediate link between Hegel and Kierkegaard, who is recognized as the first Existentialist philosopher.

10. Engels, *Ludwig Feuerbach,* pp. 32–33.
11. Sartre, "Materialism and Revolution," p. 211.
12. Ibid.
13. Ibid.
14. Ibid., p. 213.
15. Karl Marx, *A Contribution to the Critique of Political Economy,* pp. 12–13.
16. Engels, "Engels to Heinz Starkenburg," Marx and Engels *Basic Writings,* p. 411.
17. Sartre, "Materialism and Revolution," p. 213.
18. Ibid., pp. 213–14.
19. See Chapter One, p. 5 (freedom and necessity), and p. 6 (superstructure). It was remarked at the outset that here we have a contradiction in Marxist theory, and it is one that continuously creates all types of problems. It serves as a convenient loophole whenever matters become difficult in holding on to determinism. However, even if accepted as legitimate, the qualification is only a minor point in the entire theory, which is predominantly deterministic in character. The problem will be treated further in the last part of the present chapter.
20. Sartre, "Materialism and Revolution," p. 244.
21. A description of alienation given by Karl Marx

in *Economic and Philosophical Manuscripts,* "First Manuscript. Alienated Labor," in Erich Fromm, ed., *Marx's Concept of Man,* pp. 93–109.

22. Sartre, "Materialism and Revolution," p. 246.

23. Ibid., p. 253.

24. Jean-Paul Sartre, *No Exit* and *The Flies* (New York: 1952), p. 61.

25. E. L. Allen, *Existentialism from Within* (New York: 1953), pp. 91–92.

The argument that the notion of God as his own cause is self-contradictory is taken by Sartre from Nicolai Hartman.

Sartre does attempt other proofs for his atheistic principle, but they are as weak as the one given. He argues that God is not a transcendent being but only a manmade concept accounting for man's own self-transcending activity, that it is simply a case of anthropomorphism. This is one interesting genetic *explanation* for the idea of God, but as a proof it is not conclusive. Another argument is that God would be "both necessary and contingent, underived and derived, eternally immobile and temporally active . . . he is the hypothetical reconciliation of two modes of being that can never be reconciled": of the *en-soi* and the *pour-soi.* Here the problem is not in God but in Sartre's conception and division of being into two irreconcilable camps.

The above quotation from Sartre and a further exposition of these matters may be found in James Collins, *The Existentialists: A Critical Study* (Chicago: 1952), pp. 65–66.

26. Sartre, "Existentialism Is a Humanism," p. 302.

27. Lenin, *Materialism and Empirio-Criticism,* p. 170.

28. Sartre's conception of matter is best described in his semi-autobiographical novel *Nausea.* The relevant chapter has been translated separately and published in *Partisan Review,* XIII, No. 1 (Winter 1946), pp.

25–33. The parts quoted below are from this translation, pp. 30–33:

There, on those hesitant branches groping blindly about them, I was unable to seize existence in motion. This idea of transition was still man's creation, an over-clear idea. All those tiny stirrings were isolated, they were there for themselves. . . . Whatever met my eyes was a fullness. The tips of the branches swarmed with existences, with existences that were being constantly renewed and which were never born. . . . And all those existents scurring around the tree came from nowhere and were going nowhere. . . . Existence everywhere, infinite existence, superabundant, always and everywhere; existence—never limited except by existence.

Things are softness, flabbiness—yes . . . every minute I expected to see the tree trunks crumple up like burning paper, collapse and fall to the ground in a soft dark heap with deep folds in it. *They had no desire to exist;* they could not help themselves, that was it. . . . Every existent is born without reason, perpetuates itself out of inertia and dies fortuitously. . . .

Was it a dream, that enormous presence? It was there, poised over the park, tumbling from the trees, all soft, gluing up everything, a thick gelatinous mass. And was I in it, I, and the entire park? I was afraid, but above all I was furious, it seemed so stupid, so inappropriate. I despised that ignoble jelly. It was everywhere, everywhere! . . . I was very well aware that it was the World, the naked World which had suddenly shown itself, and I was choking with rage against this huge absurd being. . . . I cried out: "What a filthy mess, what a mess."

It appears that Sartre has made this literary, psychological description of the world as a nauseous mass into his philosophical theory of the world and its matter. As the Existentialist stand on God, this theory too is an *a priori* stand, although again not claiming empirical validity but only a decision and an individual experience of the world in this fashion, any other idea of the world not being "real" to the individual involved. But the question is, why does Sartre assume that his experience of the world in the manner described above is universal for all men?

29. Sartre, "Existentialism and Humanism," (London: 1952), pp. 68–69. In this and in any discussion with Sartre concerning science and scientific laws, it must be remembered that he holds the "phenomenological principle that scientific certitude refers only to what sustains universal, necessary, and essential relations," never to particular physical events and relations. This, by the way, is also an argument used by Sartre to disprove the possibility of demonstrating the existence of God or of the soul, for "metaphysical inquiries about contingent, particular modes of being and their actual causes can never attain scientific standing." From James Collins, op. cit., p. 45.

30. See page 25 for the full quotation from Marx.

31. Adam Schaff, "Stocktaking in Philosophy," *Polish Perspectives,* Vol. II, No. 11 (November 1959), p. 18. This is the same article published later under the title "Marxism and Existentialism" in *Monthly Review,* XIV, May–June 1962.

Chapter Three

1. Friedrich Engels, *Ludwig Feuerbach,* p. 54.
2. Ibid.
3. Sartre is not alone in arguing that dialectics are true for ideas but not for matter; the exiled Russian religious Existentialist, N. Berdaev, states the same thesis.
4. Jean-Paul Sartre, "Materialism and Revolution," p. 205.
5. Ibid., p. 206.
6. Ibid., p. 207.
7. Ibid., pp. 209–10.
8. Ibid., p. 210.

9. Ibid., p. 215.
10. Ibid., p. 216.
11. Ibid., p. 217.
12. Ibid., p. 210.
13. Engels, *Socialism: Utopian and Scientific*, p. 48.
14. Sartre, "Materialism and Revolution," p. 210.
15. Ibid., p. 204.
16. Ibid., p. 218 footnote.
17. Ibid., p. 205.
18. Ibid., p. 208.
19. Engels, *Socialism: Utopian and Scientific*, p. 48.
20. Sartre, "Materialism and Revolution," p. 206.
21. John Somerville, *Soviet Philosophy: A Study of Theory and Practice* (New York: 1946), p. 172.
22. Ibid., p. 173.
23. Sartre, "Materialism and Revolution," p. 216.
24. Somerville, pp. 176–77.

Chapter Four
1. Karl Marx, "Theses on Feuerbach," Marx and Engels *Basic Writings*, p. 245.
2. Jean-Paul Sartre, "Materialism and Revolution," p. 225.
3. Ibid., p. 226.
4. Norman N. Greene, *Jean-Paul Sartre: The Existentialist Ethic* (University of Michigan Press: 1960), p. 144.
5. Ibid., p. 146. Greene is quoting Sartre from *Being and Nothingness*.
6. Sartre, "Materialism and Revolution," p. 246.
7. Ibid., p. 232.
8. Ibid., p. 229.
9. Ibid., p. 234.
10. Ibid., p. 247.
11. Ibid.
12. Ibid., p. 228.
13. Ibid., pp. 235–36.
14. Ibid., p. 251.

15. Ibid., pp. 236–37.
16. Ibid., p. 251. If it is asked how a free being—since this is the existential definition of man—can be freed, Sartre replies that man "is not free and bound in respect to the same things. His freedom is like the illumination of the situation into which he is cast. But other people's freedoms can render his situation unbearable, drive him to rebellion or to death." Sartre, "Materialism and Revolution," p. 245.
17. Sartre's success in this endeavor is questionable, and even by his own admission the unity of the *pour-soi* with the *en-soi*, which would be God, is an impossibility (infra, p. 82).
18. Sartre, "Materialism and Revolution," p. 199.
19. Ibid., p. 217 footnote.
20. Ibid., p. 253.
21. Ibid., p. 255.
22. Ibid., pp. 255–56.
23. Ibid., p. 244.
24. John Somerville, "Determinism and Ethical Practice in Marxism," unpublished ms., p. 3.
25. Maurice Natanson, *A Critique of Jean-Paul Sartre's Ontology*, p. 60.
26. Ibid., p. 61.
27. Sartre, "Materialism and Revolution," p. 222.
28. Ibid., p. 223.
29. In the desire and hope for a revolutionary struggle of the workers against their oppression, Sartre implies the need for an organization, but with his ontology of personal conflict he is theoretically unable to form a useful and effective one. It is noteworthy that he does not argue for anarchy, which would be more compatible with his ontology.

Chapter Five
1. Sartre, "Materialism and Revolution," p. 219.
2. Ibid.

3. Ibid., p. 221.
4. Albert Camus, *The Rebel* (London: 1962), p. 189.
5. Ibid., pp. 190–91.
6. Ibid., p. 196.
7. Many philosophical postures of Existentialism may be traced as far back as St. Augustine, and indeed to any religious thinker who concerned himself with the individual, his salvation, his personal relation to God, to man, and to the universe, and the meaning of his knowledge, his actions, and his life.
8. Adam Schaff, "Stocktaking in Philosophy," pp. 15–16. In describing the sudden popularity of Existentialism in Poland, Schaff similarly explains the phenomenon by social reasons: the war, the suffering, and the disillusionment with Stalin.
9. Camus, p. 193.
10. Ibid., p. 222.
11. Ibid., p. 220. Camus grants Marxism scientific status in exposing social myths and the economic basis of many motivations.
12. Ibid., p. 220.
13. Pyama P. Gaidenko, "Existentialism and the Individual," *Soviet Review*, July 1962, p. 23.
14. Ibid., p. 24.
15. Ibid., pp. 17–18.
16. Norman N. Greene, *Jean-Paul Sartre: The Existentialist Ethic*, p. 162.
17. Ibid., p. 163.
18. As an aside, Dunham accuses Sartre of a predilection for using clinical cases to illustrate his philosophy.
19. Barrows Dunham, "Existentialism," *Voprosy Filosofii*, XIV, No. 9 (1960), p. 65.
20. Ibid., pp. 65–66.
21. Ibid., p. 74.
22. Ibid., p. 75.
23. Gaidenko, p. 15.

24. *Bolshaia Sovetskaia Entsiklopedia*, V. 48, p. 358.
25. Not all, but some of the traits listed must strongly remind the Soviet Marxists of their own Russian Nihilists of the last century, who, Marxists would argue, also preshadowed the doom of a society no longer fitted to new human needs.

Chapter Six

1. Ronald Grimsley, *Existentialist Thought* (Cardiff: 1955), p. 131.
2. E. L. Allen, *Existentialism from Within* (New York: 1953), p. 81.
3. Sartre, "Existentialism Is a Humanism," p. 292.
4. Grimsley, op. cit., p. 133.
5. René Marill-Albérès, *Jean-Paul Sartre: Philosopher without Faith* (New York: 1961), p. 109.
6. Grimsley, op. cit., p. 136.
7. John D. Wild, "Existentialism as a Philosophy," *Sartre: A Collection of Critical Essays*, Edith Kern, ed. (New Jersey: 1962), p. 143.
8. Ibid.
9. Ibid., pp. 143–44. The author concludes the paragraph from which these quotations come by stating that at this point Sartre "recognizes the principle of sufficient reason as something more than a peculiar habit of the *pour-soi*. Things really need a ground, but such grounds are absent. This is inconsistent with subjectivism. On the other hand, if sufficient reason is not really required, to assert that the universe is absurd is quite meaningless. Sartre's views here are either inconsistent or unintelligible." John D. Wild, op. cit., p. 144. These issues have also been alluded to in Chapter Two and particularly in footnote 28 of that chapter.
10. H. J. Blackham, "Anguished Responsibility," *Sartre: A Collection of Critical Essays*, Edith Kern, ed. (New

Jersey: 1962), p. 168. It must be remarked that Sartre can play a convenient game with alienation; for if a man willingly accepts his alienation i.e., the causes which are responsible for his alienation, then by definition he is *unconsciously* alienated. Thus it is left to the whim of the Existentialists to judge who is alienated and who is not. With the possibility of the above type of unconscious alienation they have a completely free hand in expressing any biased decisions, and by definition they are always correct.

The logic of this argument is taken from John H. Schaar's book *Escape from Authority*, p. 205, where the author speaks of Erich Fromm's use of the concept of alienation.

11. Ibid.
12. John D. Wild, *The Challenge of Existentialism* (Indiana: 1955), p. 138.
13. Ibid., p. 141.
14. Ibid., p. 150.
15. Ibid.
16. *The Republic of Silence*, A. J. Liebling, ed. (New York: 1947), p. 498.
17. Ibid.
18. Adam Schaff, "Stocktaking in Philosophy," p. 12.
19. Ibid., p. 15.
20. V. I. Svintsov, "Kritika Ekzistentsialistskikh Povetrii," *Voprosy Filosofii*, XVII, No. 1 (1963), p. 169. The article is a review of Schaff's book on Marxism and Existentialism.
21. Ibid., p. 170. Svintsov here is quoting Schaff.
22. John Lewis, "Marxism and its Critics," *The Marxist Quarterly*, II, No. 4 (October: 1955), p. 215.
23. John Somerville, "Determinism and Ethical Practice in Marxism," unpublished ms. presented at the American Philosophical Association Symposium, Western Division, 1962, p. 7.
24. John Lewis, op. cit., p. 216.

25. Pyama P. Gaidenko, "Existentialism and the Individual," p. 11.

26. Marx's Concept of Man, Erich Fromm, ed., (New York: 1961), p. 47.

27. Gaidenko, p. 15. The author quotes Marx from The German Ideology.

28. This is an argument used by John H. Schaar in his book Escape from Authority, p. 192.

29. James Collins, The Existentialists: A Critical Study (Chicago: 1952), p. 75.

30. Ibid.

31. Marjorie Grene, Dreadful Freedom: A Critique of Existentialism (Chicago: 1948), p. 70.

32. Ibid., p. 118. Grene is quoting Sartre from the French edition of Being and Nothingness, p. 480.

33. Sartre, "Existentialism Is a Humanism," p. 292.

34. Gwendolyn Bays, "Simone de Beauvoir: Ethics and Art," Yale French Studies, I, No. 1 (Spring–Summer 1948), p. 106.

35. H. J. Blackham, "Anguished Responsibility," op. cit., p. 168.

36. Sartre, "Existentialism Is a Humanism," pp. 307–8.

37. Simone de Beauvoir, "Pyrrhus and Cyneas," Partisan Review, XIII, No. 3 (Summer 1946), p. 335.

38. Simone de Beauvoir, The Ethics of Ambiguity (New York: 1962), pp. 19–20.

39. Serge Doubrovsky, "The Ethics of Albert Camus," Camus: A Collection of Critical Essays, Germaine Brée, ed. (New Jersey: 1962), pp. 77–78.

40. Ibid., p. 78.

41. Ibid.

42. Simone de Beauvoir, The Ethics of Ambiguity, p. 7.

43. Doubrovsky, op. cit., p. 76.

44. Ibid., p. 82.

45. Ibid., p. 80.

46. Albert Camus, The Rebel (London: 1962), pp. 209–10.

47. Friedrich Engels, *Herr Eugen Dühring's Revolution in Science*, p. 109.
48. R. Garaudy, "Problems of Ethics in Contemporary French Philosophy," *Voprosy Filosofii*, XIV, No. 10 (1960), p. 74.
49. Ibid., p. 77.
50. Ibid.
51. R. Garaudy, "Bourgeois Morality and Communist Morality," *Marxism Today*, III, No. 8 (August 1959), p. 245.
52. Ibid.
53. R. Garaudy, "Problems of Ethics in Contemporary French Philosophy," op. cit., pp. 64–65.
54. K. A. Schwartzman, "The Defense of Individualism in Existentialist Ethics," *Voprosy Filosofii*, XIII, No. 10 (1959), p. 24.
55. Ibid., p. 26.
56. Ibid., p. 29.
57. Schaff, op. cit., p. 16.
58. Svintsov, op. cit., p. 71.
59. Laszek Kolakowski, "The Conspiracy of Ivory Tower Intellectuals," *Essential Works of Marxism*, Arthur P. Mendel, ed., (New York: 1961), p. 350.
60. Karl Marx, *Capital: A Critique of Political Economy*, Author's Preface to the first edition (Chicago: 1906–9), p. 15.
61. Walter Odajnyk, "The Individual and Marxism," *Darshana International*, Vol. III, No. 3 (August 1963), pp. 52–53.

Chapter Seven

1. Herbert Marcuse, *Reason and Revolution: Hegel and the Rise of Social Theory* (New York: 1954), p. 262.
2. G. W. F. Hegel, *The Phenomenology of Mind* (New York: 1910), p. 249.
3. John H. Schaar, *Escape from Authority* (New York: 1961), p. 181.

4. Jean-Paul Sartre, "Marksizm i Egzystencjalizm," *Twor-czosc*, No. 4 (April 1957), p. 41. This and the following four quotations are original translations from the Polish publication *Tworczosc*, upon whose invitation the above essay was written. It appeared in full in the noted issue of the magazine; and now serves as an elaborate preface to the *Critique de la Raison Dialectique* after undergoing editorial and other changes.

5. Ibid., p. 44.

6. Ibid., p. 77.

7. Ibid., p. 78.

8. Ibid., p. 79.

9. Adam Schaff, "Stocktaking in Philosophy," p. 13.

10. Ibid., p. 16.

11. As yet no English translation is available, but an excellent outline of the book is presented in a newly published work by Wilfrid Desan. It is on the basis of Desan's book that the brief summary which follows was made. Because Professor Desan outlines Sartre's book in his own words and only occasionally relies upon direct quotations from Sartre, it is difficult at times to distinguish the speakers of the quotations used in my summary. Therefore, when possible I have identified the speaker in the text, but it would be safest to consult the relevant footnote in order to determine with certainty whether the words are Sartre's own or a paraphrase by Desan. Also, in all cases quotations with italicized words and phrases or clarifications in parentheses are in the original by Desan, none have been added or deleted by the present writer.

12. Wilfrid Desan, *The Marxism of Jean-Paul Sartre* (New York: 1965), p. 78.

13. Ibid., pp. 77–78.

14. Ibid., pp. 78–79.

15. Sartre in Desan, op. cit., p. 87.

16. Desan, pp. 84–85. In these ideas the remnants of

Sartre's previous position are clearly evident: the definition of man as a "lack" or a "need"; the *unifying*
activity of man's consciousness of his surroundings; and
the passive, inert, *en-soi* that is an obstacle for man,
now called the *antidialectic*. The difference between
these concepts as they are used in *Being and Nothingness* and in the *Critique* will develop to be that in
the *Critique* they are less psychological and more material in character.

17. Desan, op. cit., pp. 79–80.
18. Ibid., p. 80.
19. Ibid., p. 91.
20. Ibid., p. 93.
21. Ibid., p. 94. This is but a new vocabulary for the former
"look" of the Other which also served to categorize
and classify men into groups and classes. The difference between that "look" and the observation of "the
third man" is the greater emphasis in the *Critique*
upon the material and social basis that give rise to
the classification. Another important difference is the
absence of any interpersonal conflict, at least on this
simple level of observation, because the observer has
no ontological need to conquer and control the subject of his observation.
22. Ibid., p. 95.
23. Ibid., p. 96. Sartre's highlighting of scarcity and the resulting struggle for self-survival as the foundation and
the motivation for the development of groups, society,
and history, is reminiscent of Rousseau's hypothesis
on the origin of society in his "Discourse on the Origin
of Inequality."

Rousseau also begins with man's material struggle
for survival because of material scarcity in the world,
and constructs the entire society—the family, groups,
classes, the state, and history—upon this foundation.
Marx and particularly Engels are greatly indebted to
Rousseau's hypothesis, which probably had a direct

influence upon Engels' *The Origin of the Family,
Private Property and the State.*

Sartre's argument, therefore, fully conforms with the
modern French intellectual tradition on this matter,
and he could easily have come to the same conclusions as Marx and Engels through the more direct
line of his French brother, Rousseau.

24. Ibid., p. 96.
25. Ibid. Again the overtones of the Sartre of *Being and
    Nothingness* are in evidence. Conflict and its corollary
    "negation" can still be traced to the activity of man's
    consciousness. But once more the emphasis is on the
    circular and dialectical interrelationship of thought
    and activity with matter and society. Thus man ne-
    gates (makes inert, passive) nature—nature negates
    (makes inert, passive) man; man places scarcity into
    nature—nature places scarcity into man; because of
    scarcity, man negates other men—and other men, in
    turn, negate him for the same reason. It is not always
    easy to follow Sartre in this exhibition of philosophi-
    cal juggling, but his slights of hand and thought are
    convincing.
26. Ibid., p. 98.
27. It is not known what Sartre would do with wars be-
    gun for the sake of glory, religion, or any other emo-
    tional reasons not based upon material scarcity. The
    guess would be that like the Marxists with whom he
    states he is in agreement concerning historical and
    social phenomena, he would search for the material
    and economic causes of all wars.
28. Ibid., pp. 112–13. The *antiman* is the product of the
    antidialectic—the inert, passive, and unfree element
    that man encounters in the reciprocity and circularity
    of his actions upon the world and of the world's ac-
    tions upon him.
29. Ibid., p. 115.
30. Ibid., p. 116.

31. Ibid.
32. Ibid., p. 122.
33. Ibid., p. 128. Already here it is possible to recognize the beginnings of the Marxist definition of freedom —the recognition of necessity—which Sartre will openly adopt near the completion of his work. The difference between Sartre's and the Marxist definition is that with Sartre man "is not the mere helpless pawn of a dogmatic dialectic, as the Marxists would have us believe." And that unlike the Marxists, "Sartre would have us always be *aware* of the events which are operating. . . ." Ibid., p. 134 (italics in the original).

Actually this is not a correct presentation of the Marxist position on this point. Marxists do not claim that man is a helpless pawn of the dialectic, for man is also *not unfree* and may act contrary to the dialectical laws. They similarly insist upon the necessity of man's awareness of the operation of these laws. If there is any difference between Sartre and the Marxists here it would only be one of a very delicate degree on emphasis.

34. Ibid., p. 130.
35. The first part of the quotation is Desan's, the last is Sartre's in Desan, p. 131.
36. Ibid., p. 183. A number of interesting matters come to mind at this time. First, the "look" of *Being and Nothingness* is still with us. It is still the "look" of an individual that classifies and gives birth to a group, although again the material conditions are stressed, and also the cooperation of the Other is needed in the internal, practical formation of the group. Previously, the "look" was more free, more powerful in certain aspects, and particularly more arbitrary.

Also, it is evident that the *group* presently under discussion is not the same group described formerly as being constructed by the natural boundaries of space. This former group was a series; it could become a *group* in the present sense if it were, for example, opposed by another group that sought to encroach upon its territory.

Lastly, are groups formed only through the elements of conflict and opposition? Are they formed only through the activity and observation of another group as a whole, or may a single member of a group through his own activity and observation alone give cause for a group to come into being? Can any person, whether a member of a group or not, give rise to a group through his opposition to certain elements of the series? Why is it not possible to form a group without the threat of conflict or opposition but simply through a proposal of united work and harmony? Also, why should it not be possible for a powerful individual—member of no group—to give birth to groups through his beneficial influence and attitudes toward all or certain members of the series?

The presence of so many questions indicates that Sartre's theory on this point is weak. His probable answer to the above questions would be that all these are possible, but that they are not the *dominant* and most characteristic means and methods of group formation.

37. Ibid., pp. 138–39.
38. Ibid., p. 187.
39. Ibid., pp. 187–88.
40. Ibid., p. 210.
41. Ibid., p. 258.
42. Ibid., p. 208.
43. Ibid., pp. 214–15. It should be mentioned that not all groups have to pass through the different phases of the evolution: some may dissolve at the *groupe en fusion* stage, others later.
44. Ibid., p. 128.
45. Ibid.
46. Ibid., p. 298.
47. Ibid., pp. 236–37.

BIBLIOGRAPHY

Allen, E. L. *Existentialism from Within*. New York: The Macmillan Company, 1953, pp. 1–98.

Arnaud, Pierre. "Aftermath—A Young Philosopher's View," *Yale French Studies*, XVI (Winter 1955–56), pp. 106–10.

Barrett, William. *Irrational Man: A Study in Existential Philosophy*. New York: Doubleday & Company, 1958, pp. 3–57, 148–271.

Bays, Gwendolyn. "Simone de Beauvoir: Ethics and Art," *Yale French Studies*, No. 1 (Spring–Summer 1948), pp. 106–13.

Beauvoir, Simone de. *The Ethics of Ambiguity*. New York: Citadel Press, 1962.

——. "Pyrrhus and Cyneas," *Partisan Review*, XIII, No. 3 (Summer 1946), pp. 330–37.

Bieber, Konrad. *"Engagement* as a Professional Risk" (On Camus), *Yale French Studies*, XVI (Winter 1955–56), pp. 29–39.

Blackham, H. J. *Six Existentialist Thinkers*. London: Macmillan & Co., Ltd., 1952. Chapters I, V, and VII.

Boarsch, Jean. "Sartre's View of Cartesian Liberty," *Yale French Studies*, I, No. 1 (Spring–Summer 1948), pp. 90–97.

Bobbio, Norberto. *The Philosophy of Decadentism: A Study in Existentialism*. New York: The Macmillan Company, 1948.

Brée, Germaine, ed. *Camus: A Collection of Critical Essays*. Englewood Cliffs, N. J.: Prentice-Hall, 1962.

Bukhalov, I. F. "O Sootnoshenii Sub"ektivnogo i Ob"-
ektivnogo v Poznavateľnom Obraze" (On the Relation between the Subjective and the Objective in
the Cognitional Image), *Voprosy Filosofii*, XV, No.
5 (1961), pp. 124–32.

Bull, R. "Freedom," *Marxism Today*, IV, No. 7 (July
1960), pp. 220–22.

Burgelin, Pierre. "Existentialism and the Tradition of
French Thought," *Yale French Studies*, XVI (Winter
1955–56), pp. 103–5.

Camus, Albert. *The Rebel: An Essay on Man in Revolt.*
London: Penguin Books, 1962.

———. *The Myth of Sisyphus, and Other Essays.* New
York: Vintage Books, 1959.

Collins, James. *The Existentialists: A Critical Study.* Chicago: Henry Regnery Co., 1952, pp. 3–80, 188–224.

Desan, Wilfrid. *The Tragic Finale: An Essay on the Philosophy of Jean-Paul Sartre.* Cambridge, Mass.: Har-
vard University Press, 1954.

———. *The Marxism of Jean-Paul Sartre.* New York: Doubleday & Company, 1965.

Dunham, Barrows. "Ekzistentsializm" (Existentialism),
Voprosy Filosofii, XIV, No. 9 (1960), pp. 63–80.

Engels, Friedrich. *Socialism: Utopian and Scientific.* New
York: International Publishers Co., 1935.

———. *Herr Eugen Dühring's Revolution in Science.* New
York: International Publishers Co., 1934.

———. *Ludwig Feuerbach and the Outcome of Classical
German Philosophy.* New York: International Publishers Co., 1934.

Feuer, Lewis S., ed. *Basic Writings on Politics and Philosophy: Karl Marx and Friedrich Engels.* New
York: Doubleday & Company, 1959.

Fogeler, G. IA. "Kritike Ekzistentsialistskoi Kontseptsii
Sushchestvovaniia" (A Contribution to a Critique of
the Existentialist Conception of Consciousness), *Vest-*

nik Moskovskogo Universiteta, XVII, No. 5 (September–October 1962), pp. 53–63.

Fromm, Erich, ed. *Marx's Concept of Man*. New York: Frederick Ungar Publishing Company, 1961.

Gaidenko, Pyama P. "Existentialism and the Individual," *Soviet Review* (July 1962), pp. 8–25.

Garaudy, R. "Bourgeois Morality and Communist Morality," *Marxism Today*, III, No. 8 (August 1959), pp. 243–46.

———. "Problema Morali v Sovremenoi Frantsuzkoi Filosofii" (Problems of Ethics in Contemporary French Philosophy), *Voprosy Filosofii*, XIV, No. 10 (1960), pp. 64–77.

Greene, Norman N. *Jean-Paul Sartre: The Existentialist Ethic*. Ann Arbor: University of Michigan Press, 1960.

Grene, Marjorie. *Dreadful Freedom: A Critique of Existentialism*. Chicago: University of Chicago Press, 1948.

———. "Sartre's Theory of Emotions," *Yale French Studies*, I, No. 1 (Spring–Summer 1948), pp. 97–102.

———. "Authenticity: An Existential Virtue," *Ethics*, LXII (July 1952), pp. 266–74.

Grimsley, Ronald. *Existentialist Thought*. Cardiff: University of Wales Press, 1955, pp. 1–148.

Guicharnaud, Jaques. "Those Years: Existentialism 1943–1945," *Yale French Studies*, XVI (Winter 1955–56), pp. 127–46.

Hyppolite, Jean. "A Chronology of French Existentialism," *Yale French Studies*, XVI (Winter 1955–56), pp. 100–2.

Kaufmann, Walter, ed. *Existentialism from Dostoevsky to Sartre*. New York: Meridian Books, 1956.

Kern, Edith, ed. *Sartre: A Collection of Critical Essays*. Englewood Cliffs, N. J.: Prentice-Hall, 1962, pp. 1–20, 136–71.

Lenin, V. I. *Materialism and Empirio-Criticism: Critical*

Comments on a Reactionary Philosophy. Moscow: 1947.

Lewis, John. "Marxism and its Critics," *The Marxist Quarterly,* II, No. 4 (October 1955), pp. 203–16.

Liebling, A. J., ed. *The Republic of Silence.* New York: Harcourt, Brace & Company, 1947, pp. 498–500.

Lukacs, George. *Existentialismus oder Marxismus.* Berlin: 1951.

Magnan, Henri. ". . . Said Jean-Paul Sartre," *Yale French Studies,* XVI (Winter 1955–56), pp. 3–7.

Marill-Albérès, René. *Jean-Paul Sartre: Philosopher without Faith.* New York: Philosophical Library, 1961.

Marx, Karl. *Capital: A Critique of Political Economy.* Chicago: Charles H. Kerr & Company, 1906–9.

——. *A Contribution to the Critique of Political Economy.* Chicago: Charles H. Kerr & Company, 1911.

——, and Engels, Friedrich. *Manifesto of the Communist Party.* New York: Universal Distributors Company, 1948.

Mendel, Arthur P. *Essential Works of Marxism.* New York: Bantam Books, 1961.

Mounier, Emmanuel. *Existentialist Philosophies: An Introduction.* New York: The Macmillan Company, 1949.

Natanson, Maurice. *A Critique of Jean-Paul Sartre's Ontology.* Lincoln: University of Nebraska, 1951.

Odajnyk, Walter. "The Individual and Marxism," *Darshana International,* Vol. III, No. 3 (August 1963), pp. 46–56.

Patka, Frederick. *Existentialist Thinkers and Thought.* New York: Philosophical Library, 1962.

Read, Herbert. *Existentialism, Marxism and Anarchism.* London: Freedom Press, 1949.

Roberts, David E. *Existentialism and Religious Belief.* New York, 1957. Introduction, Chapters IV and V.

Sartre, Jean-Paul. *Being and Nothingness: An Essay of*

Phenomenological Ontology, trans. Hazel E. Barnes. New York: Philosophical Library, 1956.

———. *No Exit* and *The Flies*, trans. Stuart Gilbert. New York: Alfred A. Knopf, 1952.

———. *No Exit*, trans. Stuart Gilbert. New York: Alfred A. Knopf, 1947.

———. "From *Being and Nothingness:* The Caress," *Yale French Studies*, XVI (Winter 1955–56), pp. 96–99.

———. "Marksizm i Egzystencjalizm," *Tworczosc*, No. 4 (April 1957), pp. 33–79.

———. *Literary and Philosophical Essays*. New York: Collier Books, 1962.

———. *Existentialism and Human Emotions*. New York: Philosophical Library, 1957.

———. "Portrait of the Anti-Semite," *Partisan Review*, XIII, No. 2 (Spring 1946), pp. 165–78.

———. *Existentialism and Humanism*, trans. Philip Mairet. London: Noonday Press, 1952.

———. *The Transcendence of the Ego: An Existentialist Theory of Consciousness*. New York: Noonday Press, 1962.

———. *Critique de la Raison Dialectique*, I. Paris: 1961.

Schaff, Adam. *Filozofia Czlowieka: Marksizm a Egzystencjalizm*. Warsaw: 1962.

———. "Stocktaking in Philosophy," *Polish Perspectives*, Vol. II, No. 11 (November 1959), pp. 6–20. The same article appeared under the title "Marxism and Existentialism" in *Monthly Review*, XIV (May–June 1962).

———. "The Individual Determinants of Happiness," *Polish Perspectives*, Vol. V, No. 2 (February 1962).

Schwartzman, K. A. "Apologiia Individualizma v Ekzistentsialistskoi Etike" (The Defense of Individualism in Existentialist Ethics), *Voprosy Filosofii*, XIII, No. 10 (1959), pp. 20–30.

Shirokov, M., ed. *A Textbook of Marxist Philosophy*. London: V. Gollancz, Ltd.

Somerville, John. *Soviet Philosophy: A Study of Theory and Practice.* New York: Philosophical Library, 1946.

——. "Determinism and Ethical Practice in Marxism." Unpublished ms. presented at the 1962 meeting of the American Philosophical Association, Western Division.

——. "Approaches to the Critique of Soviet Philosophy," *Philosophy and Phenomenological Research,* XXIII, No. 2 (December 1962), pp. 269–73.

Spirkin, A. G. "O Prirode Soznaniia" (On the Nature of Consciousness), *Voprosy Filosofii,* XV, No. 6 (1961), pp. 118–27.

Straelen, Van H. *Man the Lonely: Preface to Existentialism.* Tokyo-London, 1952.

Svintsov, V. I. "Kritika Ekzistentsialistskish Povetrii" (A Critique of Existentialist Epidemics), *Voprosy Filosofii,* XVII, No. 1 (1963), pp. 167–72.

Thody, Philip. *Jean-Paul Sartre: A Literary and Political Study.* London: Hamish Hamilton, 1960.

Wahl, Jean. *A Short History of Existentialism.* New York: Philosophical Library, 1949.

Wild, John D. *The Challenge of Existentialism.* Bloomington: Indiana University Press, 1955.

Wollheim, Richard. "The Political Philosophy of Existentialism," *Cambridge Journal,* VII (October 1953), pp. 3–19.

GENERAL BIBLIOGRAPHY

Ames, Van Meter. "Mead and Sartre on Man," *Journal of Philosophy*, LIII (March 15, 1956), pp. 205–19.

Barnes, Hazel E. *The Literature of Possibility: A Study in Humanistic Existentialism*. Lincoln: University of Nebraska Press, 1959.

Brombert, Victor. "Raymond Aron and the French Intellectuals," *Yale French Studies*, XVI (Winter 1955–56), pp. 13–23.

Cornell, Kenneth. "*Les Temps Modernes*: Peep Sights Across the Atlantic," *Yale French Studies*, XVI (Winter 1955–56), pp. 24–28.

Dutt, K. Guru. *Existentialism and Indian Thought*. New York: Philosophical Library, 1960.

Farlow, John King and Cody, Arthur. "Creation and Human Freedom: Pico's Answer to Sartre," *Darshana*, II, No. 2 (April 1962), pp. 22–28.

Hegel, G. W. F. *The Phenomenology of Mind*. New York: The Macmillan Company, 1910.

Heidegger, Martin. *The Question of Being*. London: Vision Press, 1959.

——. *Essays in Metaphysics*. New York: Philosophical Library, 1960.

——. *Existence and Being*. Chicago: Henry Regnery Co., 1949.

Heinemann, F. H. *Existentialism and the Modern Predicament*. New York: Harper & Brothers, 1954.

Knight, Everett. *The Objective Society*. New York: George Braziller, 1960.

Marcuse, Herbert. *Reason and Revolution: Hegel and the Rise of Social Theory*. New York: Humanities Press, 1954, pp. 251–312.

Orynski, Wanda, ed. *Hegel Highlights—An Annotated Selection*. New York: Philosophical Library, 1960.

Pranger, R. J. *Sartre and Camus: Politics of Action*. Unpublished Master's Thesis. Berkeley: University of California, 1957.

——. *The Problem of Citizenship in the Action Theories of Modern Social Science and Existentialism*. Unpublished Doctoral Dissertation. Berkeley: University of California, 1961.

Rintelen, Fritz J. von. *Beyond Existentialism*. New York: Humanities Press, 1962.

Schaar, John H. *Escape from Authority: The Perspectives of Erich Fromm*. New York: Basic Books, 1961. Chapter III.

Tiryakian, Edward A. *Sociologism and Existentialism: Two Perspectives on the Individual and Society*. Englewood Cliffs, N. J.: Prentice-Hall, 1962, pp. 125–69.

Topitsch, Ernst. "The Sociology of Existentialism," *Partisan Review*, XXI, No. 3 (May–June 1954), pp. 289–304.

Voegelin, Eric. *The New Science of Politics*. Chicago: University of Chicago Press, 1952.

INDEX

ANCHOR BOOKS